Too Old – Who Says?

ISSUES FOR THE NINETIES

Volume 16

Editor

Craig Donnellan

Independence

Educational Publishers

Cambridge

First published by Independence
PO Box 295
Cambridge CB1 3XP

© Craig Donnellan 1997

British Library Cataloguing in Publication Data
Too Old – Who Says? – (Issues for the Nineties Series)
I. Donnellan, Craig II. Series
331.3'98

ISBN 1 86168 011 2

Printed in Great Britain
at Leicester Printers Ltd
Leicester, Great Britain

Typeset by
Claire Boyd

Cover
The illustration on the front cover is by
Andrew Smith / Folio Collective.

CONTENTS

Introduction

Too Old – Who Says? is the sixteenth volume in the series: **Issues For The Nineties**. The aim of this series is to offer up-to-date information about important issues in our world.

Too Old – Who Says? looks at age discrimination, the economics of ageing and retirement. The information comes from a wide variety of sources and includes:

Government reports and statistics
Newspaper reports and features
Magazine articles and surveys
Literature from lobby groups
and charitable organisations.

It is hoped that, as you read about the many aspects of the issues explored in this book, you will critically evaluate the information presented. It is important that you decide whether you are being presented with facts or opinions. Does the writer give a biased or an unbiased report? If an opinion is being expressed, do you agree with the writer?

Too Old – Who Says? offers a useful starting-point for those who need convenient access to information about the many issues involved. However, it is only a starting-point. At the back of the book is a list of organisations which you may want to contact for further information.

*****

Advice and help for older people

Introductory statistics and thoughts

In the United Kingdom in mid-1994 the total population was estimated to be 58.4 million. Those over 60 accounted for approximately 12 million of this total. This figure is rising and by the year 2031 the population of over-sixties is projected to rise to approximately 18 million. Indeed the number of people over 80 has more than doubled in the last three decades to 2.3m. There is a higher percentage of women than men in the 65-79 and 80+ age groups. Women over 60 account for 23.2% of the total female population in the United Kingdom (rising to 32% by the year 2040) and men over 65 for 13.2% of the total male population (rising to 22.7% in 2040).

There is a tendency for women to live longer than men. In 1991 women accounted for three-fifths of those aged 65 or over and among those over 85 there were more than twice as many women as men. Due to the fact that women tend to live longer a higher percentage of women than men are widowed and among those 65 or over men are more likely to be married. In 1991 only 20% of older men were widowed compared with 48% of women. 71% of older men were married compared with only 40% of women.

> *Older age can bring both burdens and pleasures; the enjoyment of retirement on the one hand, and, on the other, ill-health, low income and isolation*

According to the 1991 Census just over 3% of the ethnic minority population are over 65, that population as a whole accounts for just under 6% of the total UK population. However, this figure is set to grow rapidly over the next couple of decades since there is currently a large proportion of 'middle-aged' people within ethnic minority communities. Future service provision should be adapted to account for this.

The above figures are significant since they may have implications for the future provision of benefits, health care and the like.

Older age can bring both burdens and pleasures; the enjoyment of retirement and leisure time on the one hand, and, on the other, ill-health, low income and isolation.

Many older people still have a relatively poor standard of living and are often not recognised as making a valid contribution to society.

It is important not to consider older people as a single homogeneous group; they are all individuals with widely varying needs and interests. After all we are talking about an age range from 60 to over 100! We would not make plans for 16-year-olds by looking at middle-aged people.

Perspectives on ageism – getting the balance right

Whilst the existence of other forms of discrimination in terms of race, gender and disability are now widely recognised and indeed gaining in recognition, both legal and social, ageism is not established as a widespread form of discrimination and not taken seriously. The Government has as yet refused to legislate against ageist practices, particularly in the area of employment. This last point is proven by the recent failure of David Winnick MP's Private Member's Bill which would have made the specification of age limits in job advertisements illegal.

Stereotypes about older people still prevail. This is in some ways surprising since none of us is immune to ageing, whether through caring for older relatives or friends, or through growing older ourselves.

Part of the failure to recognise ageism is due to people's own fears and stereotypes. 'Old age' is foreseen as a time of failing health, both physical and mental, poverty, and the burden of looking after parents or grandparents.

Whilst this may be true in some cases, and we must recognise and provide for individual needs, we must also be wary of treating older people as a homogeneous and redundant grouping.

There is a danger older people will begin to conform to the stereotypes created of them!

Ageism is holding preconceived ideas and stereotypes about a person because they are 'old' (usually defined as over pensionable age) and/or excluding them from services, jobs and benefits. It may also lead to public, private or voluntary organisations failing to plan for older people because they are not considered to be a priority group.

Ageism can manifest itself in different ways. One of these ways is in the language we employ and descriptions we use of older people, including images of the way they should look and act. Ageism can also be found in the exclusion of older people, unconsciously or overtly, from certain areas of life, for example, jobs (with upper age limits), services

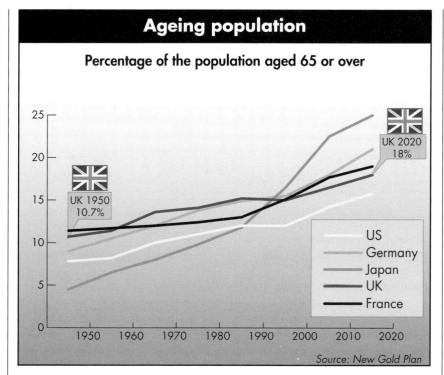

Ageing population

Percentage of the population aged 65 or over

UK 1950 10.7%

UK 2020 18%

- US
- Germany
- Japan
- UK
- France

Source: New Gold Plan

and benefits. This kind of discrimination is sometimes labelled institutional ageism.

In more subtle ways there are situations where the assistance given to an older person is well intended, but again stereotypes come into play about the person being too old to do certain activities or behave in certain ways, and in need of looking after. This attitude could be very patronising and frustrating for an active 85-year-old!

Guidelines for anti-ageist practice

- We must listen to what older people have to say.
- We must encourage a consumer voice among older people receiving care services.
- We must talk about the rights of older people and encourage a shift away from patronising over-protection towards acknow-

---

The Government has as yet refused to legislate against ageist practices, particularly in the area of employment

---

ledgement of the right to self-determination.

- We must provide services and forms of care and support that older people and their carers want rather than what we think they need.
- We must recognise that older people's needs are diverse and so must work to make services for older people as flexible and differentiated as possible.
- We must ensure that services are relevant and accessible to every older person regardless of race, religion, gender, culture or disability.
- We must work to ensure that standards, and practices of residential and domiciliary care and support promote dignity and choice for older people and their carers.
- We must avoid the stereotypes we create and perpetuate of older people and treat them as individuals.

Counsel and Care is working towards these goals

Counsel and Care produces a wide range of factsheets available on receipt of a stamped addressed envelope. A factsheet list is available on request. For further information contact our Advice Line on 0171 485 1566 between 10.30am and 4.00pm Monday to Friday.

© Counsel and Care

Campaign for older workers

Time is on my side . . . sang Mick Jagger in the sixties, and some thirty years later, he's proved it with style. With the Rolling Stones, veteran rockers well into their fifties, he stormed stages across the world in a recent, hard-rocking, sell-out tour. And yet some employers still have to be convinced about the positive benefits older workers can bring to their businesses.

Through its Campaign for Older Workers, the Department for Education and Employment is determined to drive home a message about the advantages of employing mature people. Launched in 1993, the Campaign is:

- raising the awareness of the importance of older workers;
- persuading employers to recruit, retrain and retain old workers;
- providing support and encouragement to older workers to remain active in the labour market.

Cheryl Gillan MP, minister with specific responsibility for older workers, who leads the Campaign, is firmly of the view that, 'a business which excludes workers simply on the grounds of age is depriving itself of competitive advantage in the highly competitive world markets – markets in which we must outperform those from abroad.'

She will next be on the Campaign trail in Birmingham on 3 October hosting a presentation to over 200 West Midlands employers – an important aspect of reinforcing campaign messages.

- Labour turnover statistics show that older workers stay longer, and many employers respect their commitment and loyalty. Indeed, a 45-year-old recruit is just as likely as a 20-year-old to remain with a company for 20 years.
- Older workers are just as healthy and industrious as their younger colleagues.

This debunks the notion that older workers are inflexible and unable to compete with others.

- Mature staff have a wealth of knowledge to offer, and react to given situations appropriately because they have seen it all before. They can act as mentors and guides to other employees. It is misguided to ignore the obvious advantages that come with maturity and experience.
- Older workers are just as keen to train as younger people. When the upper age limit for eligibility for the Government's Training for Work initiative was raised from 59 to 63 there was a huge positive response from people of this age group.

The Campaign's roadshows provide an excellent opportunity for employers and older workers to put the case themselves.

At the roadshow held in Glasgow on 23 June, employers from the West of Scotland heard from David Biggart, Human Resources Controller for the Britannia Life Group in Glasgow, who has introduced a strategy of encouraging the employment of older workers. One of the advantages he sees is that they tend to be more numerate which can be a great help in using computers.

Even when it comes to new technology, older workers are not daunted by computerised information systems. At Britannia Life, which is a technology-driven organisation, the older recruits' reaction to computers has presented no problem whatsoever – even when they had to learn from scratch.

The Britannia Life over-forties recruitment campaign has been very successful. It did not exclusively require recruits to be in an older age bracket but did encourage the over-forties to apply. In recruitment tests older people performed better than the norm and the company found that they had more high-quality candidates to choose from than they could use. Surveys conducted three and six months after recruitment showed that levels of satisfaction were high both among the employer and the employed.

Age has other advantages too, explained David Biggart, 'The odds are, or must be, that someone who has got thirty years' experience of being a customer knows how to handle a customer well.' As the population greys so does a company's customer profile.

The Glasgow audience heard from Tom Hall, a 46-year-old trust accountant, who found his present job after a considerable job-search including a spell at his local Jobclub. As a former bank manager Tom had a wide range of skills. Tom, like many people in a similar position, did not at first recognise the value of these skills and the fact that they can be used in other jobs and even in other industries. For Tom, the realisation came with help from recruitment consultants and this gave him the confidence to apply for work which otherwise he would not have thought available to him.

'Clearly, outdated ideas about people over 40 being near the end of their useful working lives must be challenged. Employers must judge the worth of their workforce on the value added to their business, not in terms of age.'

© *Campaign for Older Workers*

Age discrimination

From the Industrial Society

Definition

Age discrimination occurs when employers make decisions affecting procedures for advertising, recruitment, selection, promotion, training and development on the basis of individuals' age rather than their skills, abilities, qualifications and potential.

Much research is concerned with discrimination against the over-50s but job adverts frequently give age limits of 40, 35 or even 30.

Background

As the sex and race discrimination legislation of the 1970s and 1980s has become more widely accepted, people have become more aware of those groups which are not legally covered, i.e. older workers and people with disabilities.

Reasons for age discrimination are:

- Recession – organisations' reductions in the size of the workforce concentrated on early retirement first and targeted redundancy at older workers.
- Younger workers are generally cheaper to employ.
- Young employees are thought to be more flexible, more skilled in technology.
- Older workers are thought to be more costly for benefits, such as sick leave and pensions as well as salary.

However, organisations are now beginning to see the results of age discrimination:

- When older workers leave, their knowledge, skills and experience go too.
- Older employees tend to stay longer, give greater commitment and loyalty and have less absenteeism.
- Mixed age groups provide balance.

- Older customers, clients and suppliers may prefer dealing with older employees in retail, insurance, banking and other service industries.

Key facts

By the year 2050 almost a quarter of the population will be aged over 65. Yet economic activity rates for those over 50 are declining. According to government statistics:

- For men aged 50 to 64 the activity rate was 68.4% in 1995 (in 1975 the rate for men aged 55 to 59 was 94%).
- For women aged 50 to 59 in 1995 the rate was 63.9% but this rate is not declining – due perhaps to the increase in job opportunities, particularly part time, for women.
- Rates for those over retirement age drop dramatically: men – 9%, married women – 5%; and non-married women – 3%.

Of those who do work, older people are more likely to work part time. In 1994:

- Of those aged 50 to 59 more than a quarter of those who worked were part time.
- Of those aged 60 to 64, 35.5% were part time.
- For the over-65s, 70.4% were part time.
- Older people are more likely to be self-employed: of those aged 50 to state pension age, 17% were self-employed (all employees: 12.8%).

> ## By the year 2050 almost a quarter of the population will be aged over 65

A study of 4,000 job adverts by Industrial Relations Services in 1993 found that almost one-third required applicants to be 45 or under. Some specified 35 or under.

A study of the views of candidates and employers by Sanders & Sidney revealed that candidates believed career prospects started to be limited at age 42.

The cost of replacement: W.H. Smith calculates that it costs £2,500 to replace a sales assistant.

B & Q, which decided to staff an entire store with over-50s as an experiment to demonstrate the capabilities of older employees, found that staff turnover was six times lower than average, absenteeism was 39% lower and profitability turnover was up 18%. B & Q continues to recruit older workers but into mixed age group stores.

State of play

- There is no direct legislation on age discrimination in the UK. However, age-based selection for redundancy has been found to be unlawful (Walker, Nolan and Kiddy v Carbodies Ltd) and an age limit affecting more of one sex than the other could be seen as indirect discrimination under the Sex Discrimination Act 1975.
- About 100 large UK companies joined the Third Age Programme (organised by the Carnegie Foundation). Of these 20 have formally changed policies to end age discrimination.
- The Employers Forum on Age (EFA) was set up in 1996. It is a network for employers to promote mixed-aged workforces. The Industrial Society is a founder member. It provides information, auditing methods, research and so on.
- The POPE project (People of

previous experience) was set up by the Bradford & District TEC to help the unemployed over-50s get jobs. It created a register of such people and a list of employers with suitable vacancies. It matched candidates with available jobs and paid employers £2,000 for each job filled. In a year it made 110 placements.

- The age limit has now been dropped to 40, people have been given support and training and employers no longer receive the subsidy.

Best practice guidelines

Age discrimination reduces an organisation's effectiveness and, with a growing older population, gives a bad image.

- Recruitment policy should be to recruit the best staff, regardless of age. Organisations' employees should reflect the diversity of their existing and potential customers.
- To retain knowledge and experience the organisation needs to attract and retain a proportion of older employees.
- Reorganisations and redundancies should be planned so that appropriate, and not just older, employees are targeted.
- Recruitment, training, development and promotion should be on the basis of experience and aptitude, not age.

- Challenge stereotypes – many older workers like computers, welcome a challenge and want to try something new.
- Capitalise on investments in training and development for employees in all age groups.
- Avoid 'ghettos' of older workers – create mixed-age teams.
- Make sure that guidelines, policies and vision statements reflect the organisation's positive approach to age.

The above is an extract from a *Management Factsheet*, published by The Industrial Society Information service (0171 262 2401). See page 39 for address details.

© *The Industrial Society*

There are worse injustices than 'ageism'

It makes sense for companies to keep mixed-age workforces, but not at the expense of jobs for the young

By Polly Toynbee

Why, only a month ago, writing an updated version of Gulliver's aged Struldbruggs, I warned of the inevitable rise of our own gerontocracy. I predicted we would soon see a grey-power *putsch*, but I did not expect my words to be followed by action quite so soon. For today sees the launch of a major campaign to outlaw ageism. The Employers Forum on Age will unfurl its banners with the aid of Howard Davies, Deputy Governor of the Bank of England, and other assorted illuminati of industry. They want to change the hearts and minds of employers, encourage them to employ the over-fifties, and some want a legal ban on discrimination by age – a policy Labour is firmly committed to.

This is the apotheosis of the monstrous post-war baby-bulge generation. All our lives we have swept all before us with the sheer bulk of our buying power. It started in the very cradle – wasn't the NHS created in order to give birth to us

and keep us alive longer than ever? When we were teenagers, all of society had to undergo our personal teenage rebellion with us. Now as our half century hovers into view, here we come! No one is going to early-retire us forcibly, oh no. We intend to keep rocking and rolling, shaking and moving until we drop.

Today the new Employers Forum on Age will present a moving case. They estimate some one million

> *Research has shown that certain groups of customers prefer to be served by mature staff, who have both key skills and experience*

over-fifties are looking for jobs but with little success. In 1975 almost all men aged 55-65 were in work: last year that figure was down to just 60 per cent.

Most organisations set out on an orgy of downsizing during the recent recession – promoted by those pernicious kwik-fixers, the management consultants. They were the hit men who came in for a couple of weeks to shoot down short-term costs and get the hell out with very fat cheques before any consequences came home to roost. Down sizing accelerated the rate at which the over-fifties were defenestrated into early retirement. The worst case has been the finance industry, where 120,000 jobs have been lost since 1990, with an estimated 155,000 still to come by the year 2000. 'There is virtually no one left in the industry over 50,' says BIFU, the finance union.

The Employers Forum has salutary examples of where it went too far – where no one with experience was left and companies lost their memories. The skills shortage was worsened by this wanton jettisoning of experienced older workers.

Some employers are realising their mistake: Nationwide Building Society, which recently merged with Anglia, 'rationalised' its workforce and rid itself of all its over-fifties. 'But research has shown that certain groups of customers prefer to be served by mature staff, who have both key skills and experience,' they found. So now they have set about recruiting older people again.

Glaxo Wellcome found that employing the brightest and best young graduates with the freshest research background was not enough. They also needed experienced people who had seen past products through from research to delivery – older people who would 'get on with the real job in hand', without jostling for the boardroom. W.H. Smith found that workers in their twenties had a four times higher turnover than older workers, and it was costing them £2,500 a time to recruit and train each one. Now they try to hire older workers who stay longer.

Early retirement can look like an attractive option to a 50-year-old without promotion prospects. If he is earning, say, £30,000, he might be offered a £30,000 lump sum, plus a £15,000-a-year inflation-linked pension. He pays off the rest of his mortgage and sets off confidently to find another job. It need not pay as much, but just something to bring in a bit and keep him busy. No chance.

No one wants him, with all his experience, even at a cheaper rate. Young managers prefer not to supervise older people, who remind them of their parents and undermine their sense of authority. In any case, they find older people boring, incomprehensible and not fun to have around. Prejudice runs deep.

Now it must make sense for companies to keep a mixed-age workforce. They need that continuity and memory, and all the foresight that comes from remembering past disasters. But that is something employers will discover by trial and error – or maybe with the help of a new wave of mega-expensive

---

In 1975 almost all men aged 55-65 were in work: last year that figure was down to just 60 per cent

---

management consultants charged with the task of putting right what they put wrong.

But what of the concept of 'ageism' – and a whole new panoply of discrimination law, with accompanying tribunals? Is failure to employ an older person really as pernicious as discrimination on the grounds of sex, race or disability? I think not. True, you can no more help your age than your colour. But you have had your turn at being young, and they will have their turn at being old.

It is sad for fit 50-year-olds to find themselves on the scrap heap. But the chances are you have a home, your children are grown, you have a small income and your status as an ex-whatever-you-were gives you some continuing identity. Retirement is respectable and life is full of enjoyable and useful things to do outside the world of paid work. Sad, but not calamitous. Gangs of alienated unemployed 50-year-olds do not roam the streets mugging old ladies and spray-painting their tags on bus shelters.

Compare the fate of the oldies with the young who can't get their first job: even those with qualifications find it hard. They have nothing, lingering on in a perpetual adolescent limbo without status or meaning. In allocating scarce jobs, these desperate cases are in greater need than the early-retired. The Labour Force Survey lists the unemployed – registered or not – who have sought work in the last month: 16- to 19-year-olds have a 17.1 per cent unemployment rate. Fifty- to 64-year-olds have only a 7 per cent rate.

Of course, employment is not a zero-sum game. The job offered to a 50-year-old office worker would not necessarily go to an inner-city kid with a reading age of seven. Those campaigning for the rights of older workers say, aggrieved, that there is no reason why we should not care about the job prospects of both the young and the old. Why choose? But enforcing laws – or even persuading and inducing employers to retain older workers – must affect the number of jobs for the young.

It is a fine (and rarish) sight to see the best of British industry on parade for a good cause. But is the right of the bulge-baby generation to have-it-all-for-ever the best way for these great and good industrialists to expend their precious energies and sympathies?

© *The Independent*
May, 1996

Is this the right time to be tackling the age issue?

Information from the Employers Forum on Age (EFA)

Some employers may ask themselves whether they should be looking at their policies about older workers at a time when there are such grave problems for young people in finding jobs or when they themselves are continuing to cut down their own staff numbers.

None of the EFA's work is about promoting the case for older employees in preference to young employees.

There is a sound case in terms of equity for a level playing-field for people of all ages, but our principal business argument is about the benefit of a mixed-age workforce.

A well-balanced age profile will equip a business to face future demographic change with fewer concerns about skill shortages and will provide a fertile combination of skill, experience and knowledge.

It will also help a business to match the age profile of its customers

By Richard Worsley

and to operate the flexible working patterns which are increasingly required to provide a continuous service to customers, and which are often much better suited to older employees who are likely to have fewer commitments to young children and families.

> *A well-balanced age profile will equip a business to face future demographic change with fewer concerns*

For employees facing pressure to reduce numbers of employees, age will continue to be a major issue.

Those who have already achieved such reductions through early-retirement schemes may need to think again about the expertise and knowledge of the business which has gone out of the door with older employees who have accepted early-retirement packages – and the distortion of the age profile which has resulted.

Thought will be needed about how to achieve further reductions in capacity while preserving the optimum workforce for the success of the business that remains. How does that objective stand against the desire to avoid compulsory redundancy?

Neither issue is straightforward. What the EFA can do is to help employers to consider the options, to share views with others and to benefit from experience elsewhere.

© EFA
Spring, 1996

Ageism

Information from Help the Aged

To be old in Britain today is to be considered by many as 'past it', 'over the hill' or a 'has-been'. Such attitudes towards older people are widespread in a society such as ours which values youth, beauty and material possessions. For many people who are not old themselves, growing old is something to be feared. It is seen as a time of loss and withdrawal from life, rather than as a natural development which occurs gradually over time.

And yet, if you were to ask older people what they feel about being 'old', they would be likely to respond

Help the Aged

by saying that though they may look old, they feel young inside.

Many of the negative images we have about older people are perpetuated by the media, which tends to portray them as victims of crime, poverty or neglect, or as figures of fun or bemusement. If you look through any daily newspaper, most references to older people occur if they have been mugged or ill-treated, or if they have reached 100 and have become something of a celebrity.

This gives an impression that all older people are weak and vulnerable, rather than sharing the same cross-section of characteristics as the population as a whole. Television programmes, including comedies and soaps, often portray older people as 'dotty old women' like Ethel in *EastEnders* or 'miserable old men' like Percy Sugden in *Coronation Street*. It was not until the Channel 4 series *Golden Girls* that older women were seen as individual characters with the same dreams and aspirations as everyone else.

To judge a person negatively simply because of their age is to be ageist. This is akin to judging someone unfairly simply because they are black or female. However, it is only recently that ageism has been identified as equally reprehensible as racism or sexism.

Once you become aware of it, ageism is apparent in all areas of life from the derogatory way we refer to older people as geriatrics, old fogies or wrinklies to the patronising way we treat older people as if they were children and needed protecting. It also shows itself in the embarrassment and condemnation we express if an older person continues to have an interest in sex or if they prefer to dress in a style which we think is inappropriate for their age.

Ageism is at the root of some common assumptions which we make about older people: that they are all stubborn and inflexible, dependent and institutionalised, senile and sexless. These blind assumptions often display a fear and resentment about growing old and death which many of us have, but which we may be reluctant to express. Given a changing demographic situation in which one person out of every five will soon be of pensionable age, there is a strong likelihood that many of us will live to a considerable age. It is therefore in all of our interests to start challenging ageist attitudes, to ensure not only that future generations develop a more positive view of later life, but that we ourselves do not become the victims of ageism.

© Help the Aged

Keep young and employable

An anti-discrimination law alone will not put the over-40s back to work, says Jack O'Sullivan

Life used to begin at 40. But these days, as far as employers are concerned, you virtually have one foot in the grave. Those greying temples, even a few extra facial lines, and that great unalterable fact of life – your birth certificate – are all telling the same story: you are nearly past it. A survey published last year by Sanders and Sidney, employment specialists, found that 42 was the point at which most people said ageism in the workplace began to bite. Two-thirds of employees surveyed said that they had been excluded from job interviews or offers because of age.

Today, the issue finally hits Parliament, in the shape of a Bill introduced by the Labour MP David Winnick, which would ban the practice of specifying upper age limits in recruitment advertising. It is a modest proposal, long advocated by Age Concern, but unlikely to reach the statute books. Nevertheless, it is the first sign of a 'going-grey' fightback, as the baby-boomers, the generation that has grown up amid Britain's cult of youth, struggles against being consumed by its own revolution.

For those in early middle age, often saddled with mortgages and young children, employment prospects are getting to look terrifying. Whereas once, at 40, most people looked forward to another 20-25 years in work, with promotions and a generous pension based on decades of contributions, today their prospects seem bleak. Paul Gregg, an economist at the London School of Economics, estimates that most people have one promotion left in them after the age of 40 – and then they are out.

A survey found that 42 was the point at which most people said ageism in the workplace began to bite

---

The story goes that in most companies, once you are over 50, you can either be chairman or clean the toilets. Worst affected are older women, coming back to work after having children. As chief executives get younger, they are not interested in employing older underlings, whose experience might be threatening or who might prove difficult.

The practice of age discrimination is blatant. Look at any newspaper and you will find advert after advert telling older people they need not apply. Sex discrimination was banned in 1973, but the European Union recently advertised for translators aged under 32. KPMG wants to hire an accountant aged 25-30.

One senior figure in a public relations consultancy now dominated by people under 40 believes older people bring experience and good team skills to a job. But he still feels forced to take young recruits: 'We would not take on someone who was attractive and good-looking if they could not do the job. But we are an image-conscious industry. And, given that it can be 10 years before a trainee is able to give credible advice to a chief executive, we need to recruit young people.'

Diana Cornish, former managing director of Brook Street, Britain's leading employment services company, summed up most employers' attitudes in a research paper: 'Collectively these people would never dream of being offensive to a black person or belittling a woman bus-driver. Their prejudice is more widespread, socially acceptable and deadly. They believe that a person's age determines whether they can do a particular job.'

But turning the clock back, giving respect – and, most important, jobs – back to older people – is going to be hard. Several European countries and the United States outlaw age discrimination: last year a jury in Miami awarded £2.2m of damages in one case. But research published by the Department of Employment has found that such changes in the law have had no conclusive effect in improving the economic activity rates of older workers or their employment prospects.

The problem in Britain seems to be that employers have developed an entrenched fascination with youth, particularly in the expanding creative industries. 'The perception is that young people have more energy and drive and cut through the detail,' says Ashley Robinson, consultant with MacNeil, a recruitment agency for the public relations industry. 'The upbringing of people in their forties is seen as much more structured and dogged. As a result, there is a view that older people are less flexible and used to going in a straight line. People in their thirties seem to be more mercurial, in a positive sense, and prepared to take risks.'

These stereotypes are deeply ingrained. Ageism at work is part of a much wider phenomenon, according to Angela Neustatter, author of *Look the Demon in the Eye – the Challenge of Mid-Life*. 'Youth was first deified in the fifties, when teenagers were invented and youth represented something new and optimistic. And that feeling hasn't faded away. Older people have been wiped out of the picture. So people try to look young, leading to the cult of the gym, the boom in cosmetic surgery, people working harder and harder to avoid the dog barking at their heels. I was part of the group that enjoyed the youth revolution and is now paying the price for setting that agenda.'

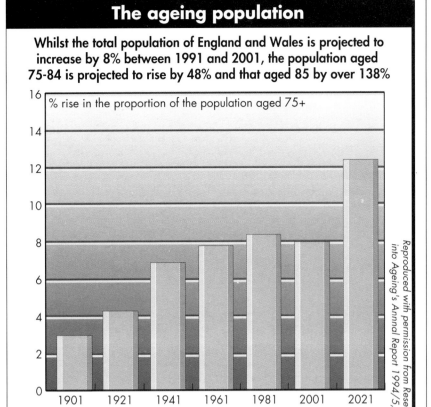

The ageing population

Whilst the total population of England and Wales is projected to increase by 8% between 1991 and 2001, the population aged 75-84 is projected to rise by 48% and that aged 85 by over 138%

% rise in the proportion of the population aged 75+

Projected

Jimmy Winterflood knows the problem. He was 50 when he was made redundant, after 27 years, from his job as product manager of a confectionery firm. 'No one was interested in someone who had maybe 10 years' work left in them. They wanted someone younger, who would in time fill senior positions.'

But he is living proof of the fallacy that old workers are no use. He volunteered to work for British Executive Services Overseas, which specialises in sending skilled middle-aged people to top positions in Third World countries. 'I've been all over the world. I'm just back from Bangladesh, where I was sorting out management problems in a biscuit and bread company. Developing countries revere people over 50, who have a lifetime of experience. I would rather give my knowledge away for nothing to someone who appreciates it than sit at home in a country that does not seem to want it.'

Demographic changes demand a rethink of ageist prejudices. There are simply not enough young people: a million fewer 16-19-year-olds now than a decade ago. By 2031, half the British population will be over 45. Recently 90 large companies, including Marks & Spencer and the Royal Bank of Scotland, agreed to oppose age discrimination.

Yet there is no indication of a waning in the power of the youth cult that has so devalued the contribution of older people. Tony Blair speaks evangelically of the need to make Britain a young country again, a message that hardly chimes with population trends. Equally, the heralding of an enterprise economy and a culture of insecurity seem to be at odds with values associated with age. This is a hostile environment in which youth thrives best.

It may be that we need a cultural shift as great as the post-war dispensation in favour of the young. This would require the baby-boomers to make a historic U-turn, and put youth back in its proper place. They would, like Dorian Gray, have to recognise the truth and abandon their own 'youthful' self-image which is now so oppressive. Unless they have the courage to do so, it is hard to see how society will overcome the prejudice, marginalisation and economic decline that a majority will soon face.

© *The Independent*
February, 1996

Age works

A message to employers

It makes no business sense . . .

Age discrimination to a greater or lesser extent exists in some form across industry, commerce and the public sector.

It is therefore not surprising that many older people – 'as old as 40 in some sectors of the job market' – come up against age discrimination when seeking employment.

Those from within your own industry suggest that:

- Up to 60% of vacancies contain an age-related restriction and 74% of employers actively recruiting are seeking candidates in the 21-30 age range. (Survey of The Institute of Employment Consultants' members, December 1994)
- As many as 37% of personnel managers admit to use of age limits in recruitment (Manchester Metropolitan University survey of Institute of Personnel & Development members, 1994)

As you know, discrimination can occur at all points of the selection and recruitment process. It can be overt – for example, contained within a job specification received. It can be hidden – for example, exclusion at the shortlist or interview stages.

Business does not benefit by practising age discrimination.

Employers and recruiters, as well as individuals in work or seeking employment, lose out. Leaving older workers out of the frame simply doesn't make any sense – business or otherwise !

Your industry says that:
'75% of recruitment consultancies said they could fill a vacancy much more quickly if there were no age criteria. Filling a vacancy quickly means the job gets done, money is saved and productivity boosted. There are no losers. The Recruitment and Employment Services industry has an incentive to do all it can to combat age discrimination in employment.' Christine Little, Chief Executive, Federation of Recruitment and Employment Services

Age discrimination makes no sense for your business. The faster vacancies are filled the greater the capacity to increase your business, satisfying the client employer, attracting more people seeking employment, raising your revenue and the profitability of your agency or business.

Some of the more important reasons for being positive about older workers are:

Skill shortages – Unless employers take a more realistic approach to age, certain types of jobs will take longer to fill, to the detriment of everyone.

Waste – Imposing age bars on recruitment means the best person for the job may be missed.

Professionalism – Age discrimination is not compatible with good recruitment practice.

Ageing society – By the year 2000, 40% of the workforce will be over 45. There will be fewer younger workers. Over the next ten years, the number of people under 35 is predicted to fall from 12.4m now to 10.9m in 2006.

Say no to age limits . . .

A growing number of your colleagues and competitors appreciate that age discrimination is damaging and have taken action. Here are some examples of the steps they have taken:

Abacus Recruitment has eliminated all age references from its candidate database.

If an employer mentions age limits, **Tate Appointments** asks why. *'If we felt the reason wasn't valid, we try to suggest why someone of a different age group could do the job equally well.'* Gill Rebbeck, Consultant

'If the employer seems keen on age limits we try to open it up. When we have taken all the details, we always say something like "but I take it if a candidate had all the skills) you'd be happy to see someone more mature, wouldn't you?"' Sally Collins, Area Manager, Kelly Services

Brook Street carries no age restrictions or language implying age in job advertisements. A range of ages is reflected in their publicity materials.

Recruit specifically mentions age in the equal opportunities statement on their terms and conditions of business leaflet.

Manpower plc has facilities to help people identify their skills, aptitudes and interests with a view to career change or development and provides free, no strings attached, training or retraining. They have great success with people aged 45 upwards who want to retrain.

Ecco has an agency dealing exclusively with mature candidates – AgeWorks.

Reed significantly reduces fees when placing permanent workers over 50.

'We halve the fee. We do this to ensure there's a real reason to encourage employers to look at CVs of people over 50.' Katy Nicholson, Public Relations Manager

Hays Accountancy Personnel believes in promoting the benefits of the older candidate to all their clients.

● The above is an extract from *Age Works*, produced by the Department for Education and Employment.

Ageism ban ushers in new jobs era for older workers

By Tony Hazell,
Careers Correspondent

Older workers have won another battle against age discrimination. Agencies responsible for 90 per cent of recruitment advertising have signed a pledge to banish age limits.

More than a third of advertisements include age limits creating a frustrating barrier for tens of thousands of older workers who have the skills, experience and enthusiasm demanded by bosses, but are ruled out due to age.

Discrimination can cut in from the mid-30s in sales, information technology, marketing and financial services. In many other management jobs the barriers go up in the 40s.

But by the end of the century at least one in three of the workforce will be aged 40 or over.

Under the voluntary code, the agencies will no longer suggest that employers put age limits in advertisements.

When employers ask for age limits the agency will ask why it is necessary. If the employer insists on the limit the agency will ignore it when processing applications.

Agencies signed up include the biggest names such as Austin Knight, Bernard Hodes, Macmillan Davies, PA Advertising and Riley Advertising. They place job advertisements for major employers such as Glaxo, Halifax Building Society, Debenhams, the armed forces and the Government.

The initiative was organised by the Carnegie Third Age Institute and the magazine *People Management*.

'I think we could get age out of most job advertising fairly quickly,' says Anne Riley, chief executive of Austin Knight. 'What could be more difficult is stopping employers discriminating when they process applications.

'But with skill shortages in many areas, especially IT, they will have to recognise that age is no longer a legitimate factor in recruitment.'

The move was welcomed by politicians. 'Age has no bearing on a person's ability to do a good job,' says Education and Employment Minister Cheryl Gillan.

Shadow Employment Minister Ian McCartney says: 'There is an overwhelming business case for employing a balanced workforce.'

People like Paul Lewis, 54, could benefit. He has been job-seeking since being made redundant four years ago. 'I have applied for about 300 jobs and could paper my walls with the rejection letters,' he says.

'I have tried networking, telephoning, the national and trade press, agencies and headhunters. I have been for computer training and even paid £8,000 to a career consultant, all to no avail.'

Mr Lewis, who lives in London, has a working life's experience in the clothing and textile industry. He joined textile merchant Holland and Sherry in 1959 and by 1979 had become joint managing director. He was chairman of two Savile Row tailors and worked for Selfridges before joining Aquascutum in 1987 where he earned £39,500 a year putting together a US merchandising collection.

'People like me would happily work for half our former salaries, but instead we are thrown on the garbage heap,' he says.

Richard Goldie, chief executive of Macmillan Davies, says that in order to get the right skills, employers will have to ignore an applicant's age.

'By challenging prejudice we are seeking to change the attitude of the more traditional employers who need to realise that over the next decade the number of people over 35 looking for work will rise, while men and women aged 25-34 available for work will decline,' he says.

Richard Worsley, director of the Carnegie Third Age Programme, says: 'Winning the support of so many recruitment advertising agencies could be a crucial turning-point in exposing the fallacy that anyone can tell from a person's age whether they have what it takes to employ them.'

© *Daily Mail*
July, 1996

I SUPPOSE YOU REALIZE, THOMPKINS, THAT GROWING OLD IS AGAINST COMPANY RULES?

MANAGING DIRECTOR

Ken Pyne

The poverty debate

Elderly people are a section of the population traditionally seen as 'poor'. This perception has a potential impact on government policy: is the state retirement pension generous enough? What criteria should be used to uprate it? Should the state retirement pension remain the main source of income for elderly people, or should private provision (personal and occupational pensions) be encouraged?

There is, however, no agreement about how 'poverty' should be defined. In May 1989, John Moore, then Secretary of State for Social Security, caused a furore by declaring that poverty in Britain no longer existed. He argued that absolute poverty, such as can be seen in developing countries, did not exist in Britain, and that for the 'poverty lobby' to insist that 'the rich are getting richer and the poor poorer' was to redefine 'inequality' as 'relative poverty'.

A second strand of argument is to ridicule the use of benefit levels as a measure of this 'relative poverty'. If people receiving Income Support are accounted 'poor', then each time benefit levels are increased, more people will fall below the threshold and be eligible to claim, and the more 'poor' people there will be. The Government's generosity, by this definition, is seen as creating poverty.

It should be remembered that the term 'retired population' spans an age range of four decades, from the early retired, fit person of 55 with a large occupational pension to a single woman of 85, surviving on Income Support. The 'retired population' is anything but homogeneous. However, despite these arguments, looking at the position of the retired population as a whole still gives the overall impression of a majority living on very limited means.

● In 1994, nearly 1.6 million pensioners and their dependants in Great Britain were receiving Income Support payments. It has been estimated that between 580,000 and as many as 840,000 pensioners may be eligible for Income Support, but are not claiming it. Moreover, around 1.4 million pensioner households (an estimated 2.3 million people) not eligible for Income Support in 1994 still had sufficiently low incomes to qualify for Council Tax Benefit.

● In 1991/92, 40% of single pensioners and 28% of pensioner couples had incomes which were less than half average income. 67% of single pensioners and 59% of pensioner couples had incomes which were less than 80% of the average (Households below average income: a statistical analysis 1979-1991/92, table F1(AHC)).

● Only one-third of people aged 65+ pay income tax (House of Commons

Hansard, 11.06.93, col. 364). This means that two-thirds (some 6 million people aged 65+) have an annual income of less than £5,090 (single people) or £12,546 (for a married couple).

● In MORI's 1990 survey on poverty in the UK for London Weekend Television's series *Breadline Britain 1990s*, retired people were one of the groups most likely to be 'poor'. MORI used a relative notion of 'poverty' in the survey, one based on a consensus. People not able to afford three or more items deemed necessities by a majority of those interviewed were classed as 'poor'.

● In the survey 'Attitudes to Ageing', produced by British Gas in 1991, 31% of pensioners said they sometimes struggled to pay for necessities.

Are retired people becoming better-off?

The Government has stated that since the 1970s, the income of pensioners has increased quite substantially in real terms, as the earnings of the working population have increased. The figures have been disputed, however, with others claiming that the real increase in pensioners' incomes has been small ('Pensioners' incomes and expenditure 1970-85', Dawson and Evans, *Employment Gazette* May 1987; and 'Poverty in official statistics: two reports', Johnson and Webb, Institute for Fiscal Studies 1990).

Up to 1980, pensions were uprated annually by either the increase in prices using the Retail Price Index (RPI), or the increase in earnings, whichever was the greater. Since 1980, pensions have been uprated simply in line with the increase in the RPI. This has resulted in the basic-rate pension for a couple dropping from 31.5% of average male earnings in 1979 to 24.7% of average male earnings in 1991 (Disney and Whitehouse, *Fiscal Studies*, 12(3), August 1991). Had the link with the increase in earnings been maintained, the basic pension in 1993/94 would be worth £18.45 more for a single person and £29.50 more for a couple (Hansard, 6.12.93, col. 12).

Moreover, the RPI measures the price of goods and services used by the 'average family'. Pensioner households are not 'average families'. A single-pensioner household, relying mainly on state benefits, spends a considerably higher proportion of income on essentials like food and fuel than the average family does: 25.2% of income on food, compared with 17.8%, and 11.1% on fuel, compared with 4.6% (Family Spending 1994-1995, tables 1.1 and 4.1). Any rise in the cost of these essentials (for example through the recent imposition of VAT on domestic fuel) will therefore affect single older people far more than the RPI implies.

Occupational pensions are said to be making a great difference to pensioners' incomes, as more and more people are retiring with more than the state pension: in 1990/91, 61% of pensioner households had income from occupational pensions. However, the average amount received from these pensions was £60.80 a week; that is just over £3,000 a year. Moreover, although recently retired households do have higher occupational pensions than the average pensioner household, the difference is not large: an average of £71.60 per week as opposed to £60.80 (Pensioner Income Results 1979-1990/91, DSS, table 3).

The dramatic rise in property prices during most of the 1980s is also said to have greatly increased the assets of retired home owners. Although commercial 'equity-release' schemes do exist, they are not always an appropriate option, leaving the problem of the 'house-rich, cash-poor' elderly home owner.

● The above is an extract from a factsheet *The Older Population*, published by Help the Aged. See page 39 for address details.

© Help the Aged

Income

Information from Help the Aged

The first state pension in Great Britain was introduced in 1908 by Lloyd George. It was a flat rate of 5 shillings; it was 'means-tested' and only paid to those over 70! National Insurance contributions paid by everyone in employment to pay for a state pension were introduced in 1948 – little more than 40 years ago.

How much is the state retirement pension worth today?
From April 1996, a single person receives £61.15 a week, if they have paid the set amount of contributions during their working life. A couple will receive £97.75 a week if a married woman has not paid enough contributions to qualify for a pension in her own right. People who have paid higher National Insurance contributions, for instance through the state earnings-related pension scheme (SERPS), will receive a higher pension.

Many people have extra sources of income, from a pension from their old job (an 'occupational pension') or from savings and investments. Often, however, these extra sources of income are very small: in 1988, in more than half of cases, an occupational pension was worth only about £20 a week or less. This means that a great many people still rely very heavily on the basic state pension as the main part of their income:

● 54% of pensioner households get at least three-quarters of their income from state benefits (House of Commons Hansard, 21.02.1991, col. 262W)

If a pensioner's income is very low, it is possible to claim another state benefit, Income Support, to bring their income up to a certain level. These levels vary, depending on the age of the person, and are shown below.

Age	60-74	75-79	80+
Single	£67.05	£69.20	£73.80
Couple	£104.10	£107.10	£112.25

For example, a single pensioner aged 69, whose only income was the state retirement pension of £61.15, would receive an Income Support payment of £5.90 a week to top their income up to £67.05.

Are pensioners poor?
It has been argued that pensioners are getting increasingly well-off. This may well be true for those who retire with a large occupational pension, but it is far from the case for those who rely heavily on state benefits. Those who retired a long time ago, particularly older women, can still find great difficulties in making ends meet.

Between April 1993 and April 1994, over 1.5 million pensioners received Income Support. It is estimated that a further 580,000 to 840,000 pensioners were entitled to receive Income Support, but did not claim it. This gives an idea of the number of people living on the amounts shown in the table opposite.

© Help the Aged
September, 1996

Poverty awaits those who fail to save up for their retirement

The state's role

Old age lived in poverty is set to become the reality for a large number of pensioners over the coming decades.

First, as the state pension is uprated each year in line with prices, rather than incomes, the basic pension is declining steadily relative to average earnings – ignoring the reality that, as the standard of living rises, so does society's view of what is an acceptable standard for the poor.

Unemployment has been above two million for most of the past 15 years and more individuals coming to retirement will have experienced at least some period out of work.

There is greater inequality of earnings in work, and short-term contracts and job mobility are increasingly prevalent. There is a growing risk that an increasing proportion of the population will have been unable to contribute to an employer's or personal pension sufficiently to lift them away from dependency on the state pension for an important part of their income.

And others, more able to make their own provision, have yet to wake up to the reality of the falling value of the state pension and the need for increased private provision to realise the standard of living in retirement which they expect.

Put simply, if nothing is done there will be two outcomes. First, inequality of income in old age will become more marked – continuing a trend already apparent in the 1980s. Second, means testing will increase as more pensioners depend on Income Support.

But it would be unrealistic to propose that the link to earnings can simply be restored, because this would require a much higher level of National Insurance contributions. Moreover, much of the benefit of the linkage to earnings would accrue to those who are already able to achieve a good level of pension provision outside the state scheme.

So it is questionable whether a universal scheme will still be appropriate as the number of pensioners rises. The main argument against any change from the universal principle is that the incentive to

> *There is a growing risk that an increasing proportion of the population will have been unable to contribute to an employer's or personal pension sufficiently*

provide for old age is much reduced if entitlement to state provision becomes means tested.

Against this, however, it has to recognised that disincentives to save will in any case affect more people as dependence on Income Support grows. And a cynical view might be that there will always be some incentive to save, as there is always suspicion that the state will renege on its promises.

A reform which challenges the universal entitlement with the aim of raising the floor for pensioner incomes therefore seems inevitable. An alternative future in which inequality of income for those of working age is extended into old age is an uncomfortable one.

© *The Guardian*
September, 1996

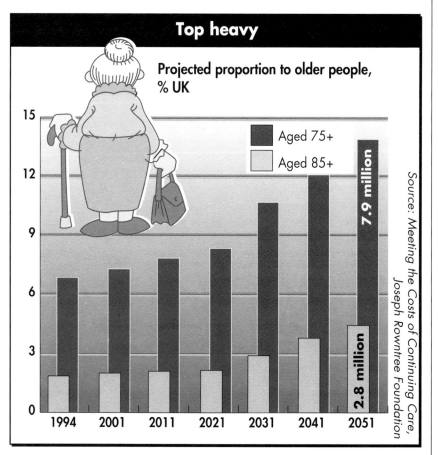

Top heavy

Projected proportion to older people, % UK

- Aged 75+
- Aged 85+

7.9 million

2.8 million

1994 2001 2011 2021 2031 2041 2051

Source: Meeting the Costs of Continuing Care, Joseph Rowntree Foundation

Europe faces a grey future

Stephen Bates on the ageing EU population

The European Commission yesterday unveiled a striking picture of what Europe will be like in 30 years, with an ageing population and migration southwards towards the sun.

The report projects an extra 37 million in the number of people aged over 60 – an increase of nearly 50 per cent. There will be 113.5 million pensioners in the European Union, nearly a third of the population.

Those of working age, between 20 and 59, will shrink by 13 million and there will be nearly 10 million fewer children and teenagers, representing an 11 per cent decline in the numbers under the age of 20.

The survey makes clear that some countries will suffer enormous demographic and social pressures as a result of the changing balance of their populations.

Ireland will see a 67 per cent increase in its retired population and a 25 per cent drop among the young, while Germany will have to cope with a 51 per cent rise in its over-60s, with a 13.5 per cent drop in its working-age population and a 12 per cent decline in the number of its young people.

The United Kingdom will have a 43.6 per cent increase in the population aged over 60 between now and 2025, a 2.8 per cent decline in the working population and an 8.2 per cent drop in the under-20s.

Statisticians have known for some time that the population is ageing, but the latest figures show more starkly how great the shift in the balance of the population will be by 2025 – and what the consequence will be for social welfare provision.

The 32-page report by the European Commission's statistical office warns: 'The labour market will have to adapt to a different kind of demand, principally in the fields of education, housing, health, transport and leisure.

'This will have to be done precisely at a time when those producing the resources needed by the economy are steadily decreasing in number and when the future generations (who will have to be highly educated and trained if growth is to be achieved) will also be fewer and fewer in number.

Some countries will suffer enormous demographic and social pressures as a result of the changing balance of their populations

---

'All aspects of social and family life will thus be dominated by the needs of older people. What concessions will the elderly be prepared to make to the younger generations and how will the latter finance pensions?

'There can be no doubt that the principle of solidarity between generations will emerge as a key factor in the adjustments which will have to be made.'

But the report warns that changing social patterns, including the decline of the family unit, may make it much more difficult to accommodate the generational shift.

It says: 'Not only are certain social protection systems based on the traditional concept of the family model . . . but some of them also presume the provision of family support for the very old. Given the context of family changes, the possibility for families to assume such support could necessitate certain adjustments to the labour market and the organisation of social protection.'

The report predicts that increasing numbers will head for the southern coastal districts of Europe because of their better climate and associated industrial development.

It also argues that, while depopulation of city centres is likely to continue, the suburbs will grow and populations will be concentrated along the traffic corridors linking major cities.

Across Europe, Scandinavia has seen an upturn in fertility levels and increases in birth-rates in the last 10 years. The central EU countries,

including the UK, the Low Countries and France, have seen levels of fertility decline over the last 20 years below what is needed to maintain population levels.

Fertility rates in Germany and Austria – where the post-war baby boom took place earlier than elsewhere – have also been very low. Southern Europe and Ireland have seen a sudden drop in fertility levels and consequently are likely to have the largest disproportions in their elderly and young populations.

Although the decline in the young population might lead to some savings in education and welfare systems, these are likely to be outweighed by increasing costs associated with the elderly. 'The fall in the number of children in the past has not automatically produced an equivalent fall in per capita expenditure on child care and education.'

To counter the decline in the indigenous population, the report estimates that net immigration into EU member states would have to rise from its current level of half a million a year to as much as 7 million.

The report argues that the scope for couples to decide the spacing and number of their offspring freely and independently has led to a drop in fertility. Social and medical progress has permitted a longer life span in better health. The report claims other surveys show Europeans now want more children than they actually have.

It adds: 'Whereas life expectancy was initially achieved by cutting infant mortality, further improvements are now principally due to falling mortality at advanced ages: death is occurring later and later. Nowadays children who have reached their first birthday are unlikely to die before the age of 60.'

Of the over-80s it says: 'Thirty years from now, there will be two or three times as many people in this age category as there are now, bringing with it a proportional increase in the specific infrastructure needed to cope with their particular requirements'

© *The Guardian*
March, 1996

Why didn't you save more, Grandpa?

Few fit and healthy young people spare a thought for how they might pay for the meals on wheels, or the residential nursing home 50 years down the road. About one in five people are likely to need long-term care once they retire. But planning for that eventuality is not high on most people's lists of priorities.

Our population is ageing; the burden of long-term care is growing. According to a report released yesterday by the think-tank IPPR and the economics consultancy London Economics, the number of people in need of long-term care will rise from 2.2 million today, consuming 6,600 hours of care a year, to 3.3 million, needing 9,700 hours in 2031.

The current system is likely to come under increasing strain. At the moment only those with assets worth less than £16,000 are eligible for government support. Everyone else is obliged to fund their own care – and, if necessary, to sell their assets (usually their house) to do so. This year 40,000 people will be forced to sell their houses to pay for care. Relatives expecting to inherit a nest egg are losing out. Conservative backbenchers claim to have post-bags full of complaints.

All would be well if everyone decided to take out insurance to finance their care, should they need it. The trouble is that most people cannot afford to do so or will not. Given a choice, most people would prefer to spend their current income rather than put it by to guard against a risk at some distant point in the future. So a voluntary insurance system is full of pitfalls. Yet expecting the taxpayer of 2031 to fork out for the steeply rising costs of their grandparents' care seems increasingly unfair.

So this is the trap that we are in: we expect government to make sure the supply of long-term care will rise to meet demand and yet we baulk at the prospect of paying more taxes. There are two escape routes. The first would be a sweeping reform to introduce compulsory insurance for long-term care for everyone. It does not matter whether this is administered by the state or the private sector. The purpose would be to make the current working generation save for their future likely needs. The size of the insurance premium would depend on ability to pay; the state would step in to build up credits for the unemployed. It would not be a tax; it would be saved to pay for future care.

The second approach would be to encourage the creation of a new private insurance market for those with assets, who could pledge a portion of those assets to fund an insurance policy for their old age. The state would continue to provide for those who cannot afford their own care.

Whatever the details of policy, the fact is that as a society we will have to devote more resources in the next 40 to 50 years to caring for the elderly and ill. The state cannot afford to stand by and just hope people will provide for themselves, but any intervention would be extremely politically sensitive. We need new and imaginative schemes, of the kind outlined by the IPPR, to bring together the public and the private – and we need to start work on them soon.

© *The Independent*
January, 1996

Older people in the United Kingdom

Some basic facts

This information has been developed as a result of the many enquirers who contact Age Concern England each year needing statistics on a wide range of topics of relevance to older people. It is updated at least annually. It gives information about older people throughout the United Kingdom but, because administrative structures are different, in some cases statistics are given for Great Britain (i.e. England, Scotland and Wales only). These figures are marked with the symbol (GB).

Unless otherwise stated the figures are for 1994 (which is the most up-to-date year with comparable data) and refer to people of pensionable age (i.e. men aged 65 and over and women aged 60 and over).

Following each paragraph a number denotes the source. A list of sources is given at the end of the article.

In the United Kingdom there are over 10 million older people:

8,893,000	in England
911,000	in Scotland
580,000	in Wales
246,000	in Northern Ireland[1]

An ageing population

In 1994, the population of the United Kingdom based on mid-year estimates was 58,395,000. Of this figure, 10,630,000 people were over pensionable age:

6,920,000 – were women aged 60 and over (of whom 5,476,000 were aged 65 and over)
3,710,000 – were men aged 65 and over
9,186,000 – were people aged 65 and over
3,963,000 – were people aged 75 and over
1,011,000 – were people aged 85 and over[1]

In 1994, almost two-thirds of people aged 75 and over were women: 2,615,000 women compared to 1,347,000 men. And over three-quarters of those aged 85 and over were women: 759,000 were women compared to 251,000 men.[1]

In 1993 a man of 60 could be expected to live for another 17.8 years and a woman of the same age for 21.9 years.[2]

In 1994, in the United Kingdom, 8,000 people (7,000 women and 1,000 men) were aged 100 and over. In 2031 it is estimated that 28,000 women and 6,000 men will be in this age group.[3]

Either from choice or because they cannot find employment, people are retiring earlier. In 1994, only 51% of men aged 60-64 and 69.3% of women aged 45-59 were working. The projections for 2006 are 49.1% of men and 72.6% of women.[4]

(GB) In 1995 people from ethnic minority groups represented just under 6% of the population. Of these:

7.2% of the Indian population were aged 60 and over
4.3% of the Pakistani/Bangladeshi population were aged 60 and over
7.2% of the Black population (including Caribbean, African and other Black people of non-mixed origin) were aged 60 and over[5]

An ageing population in the future

The number of people of pensionable age (65 for men and 60 for women) is projected to grow fairly slowly for the remainder of the century, rising by around 2% over the next 10 years.[6]

In 2031, the population of the United Kingdom is projected to total 62,241,000. Of this figure 14,292,000 will be over pensionable age (almost 24% of the population).[7]

Number of centenarians

Average UK life expectancy in 1982 for men was 72.9 years (Eurostat 1992). Increases in life expectancy have not been matched by a proportionate improvement in health and mobility.

Source: OPCS

Note: the change in the state retirement age to 65 for both sexes will be phased in between April 2010 and March 2020.

The number of people aged over 75 and the proportion they form of the total population is projected to double over the next 50 years, while the number aged 90 and over will have increased fivefold.[6]

The projected change in the population is as follows:

1992   4,035,000 aged 75 and over
         936,000 aged 85 and over

2001   4,505,000 aged 75 and over
        1,235,000 aged 85 and over

2011   4,803,000 aged 75 and over
        1,468,000 aged 85 and over[7]

Income

The basic pension from April 1996 – April 1997 is: £61.15 for a single pensioner, and £97.75 for a couple (claiming on the husband's contributions) per week.

From April 1996, the main weekly Income Support rates are as follows:

for people aged 60-74,
    £67.00 for a single pensioner and
    £104.10 for a couple

for people aged 75-79,
    £69.20 for a single pensioner and
    £107.10 for a couple

and for those aged 80 and over, or who are ill or disabled and aged 60 and over,
    £73.80 for a single person and
    £112.25 for a couple, per week

(GB)   Average adult weekly full-time earnings were £336.30 in 1995.[8]

In 1993, 51% of pensioner households depended on state pensions and benefits for at least 75% of their income.[9]

(GB)   In May 1995, 1,781,000 people aged 60 or over (single people or couples) were receiving Income Support because of their low income.[10]

The Department of Social Security estimates that in 1993/94 between 27% and 35% of pensioners who were entitled to Income Support, between 7% and 13% who were entitled to Housing Benefit, and between 24% and 33% entitled to Council Tax Benefit did not claim.[11]

Where the head of a household is aged 65 and over, a higher proportion of money is spent each week on housing, fuel and food (41.5% of expenditure) than in other households (38.2%).[12]

The most severe deprivation is experienced by pensioners living alone who are mainly dependent on state pensions. 52.8% of their expenditure goes on housing, fuel and food.[13]

The definition of expenditure on housing changed with the 1992 figures. Thus the data in the above two sections cannot be compared with earlier years.

In 1994/95, one-adult retired households mainly dependent on benefits spent 11.1% of their average weekly household expenditure on fuel, light and power compared with 4.8% for single non-retired households.[13]

Living alone

(GB)   In 1994, in the 65-74 age group, 18% of men and 39% of women lived alone, and 33% of men and 59% of women aged 75 and over lived alone.[14]

(GB)   In 1994, of people aged:

65 to 75	75 and over
75%	60% of men were married
51%	23% of women were married
12%	32% of men were widowed
37%	64% of women were widowed[15]

In 1994/95, of pensioners mainly dependent on state pensions and living alone:

73.6%   had central heating, compared to 84.3% of all households

9.9%   had a car, compared to 69% of all households

85.7%   had a telephone, compared to 91.1% of all households

59.0%   had a washing machine, compared to 89% of all households.[16]

Carers

(GB)   Between 1985 and 1990 the proportion of carers whose main dependant was aged 85 or over increased from 15% to 20%.
In 1990, 57% of carers had dependants over 75 compared with 53% in 1985.
In 1990, as in 1985, more than two-thirds were looking after female dependants.[17]

(GB)   Amongst the carers in 1990 who devoted at least 20 hours a week to caring:

44%   were aged 46-64
28%   were aged over 65[18]

Sources of data used:
1 *Population Trends* (PT), Summer 1996, tables no. 5 and 6.
2 *Social Trends* (ST), 1996, table no. 7.3.
3 Govt. Actuary's Dept, 1994-based *National Population Projections*.
4 ST, 1996, table no. 4.4.
5 ST, 1996, table no. 1.7.
6 1992-based *National Population Projections*.
7 *Ibid*, appendix 1.
8 *Labour Market Trends*, March 96, table no. 5.6.
9 *House of Commons Hansard*, 11/7/96, col. 297W.
10 Dept of Social Security *Income Support Statistics*, May 95.
11 *Income-related benefits: estimates of take-up in 1993/94*, DSS.
12 *Family spending: a report on the 1994/95 Family Expenditure Survey* (FES), table no. 2.1.
13 *Ibid*, tables no 4.1 and 4.2.
14 *General Household Survey* (GHS) 1994, table no. 2.31.
15 *Ibid*, table no. 2.22(b).
16 FES, op cit, table. no. 9.4 and 9.5.
17 OPCS Monitor SS92/2, 17/11/92, table no. 13.
18 *Ibid*, table no. 17.

● The above is an extract from *Older People in the United Kingdom*, published by Age Concern. See page 39 for address details.

Your pensions options

Information from the Trades Union Congress

Pensions are an important part of your employment rights. The benefits from a pension will provide the money you will live on in retirement – which may last for 15 years or more.

So it is important that you know about your entitlements and that you start thinking about pensions. The sooner you act, the more money you will have to live on when you retire.

This article tells you:
what your basic pensions rights are; what the choices are; how much each type of pension will give you; why you should start thinking about your pension as soon as you start work; and to think carefully about the choices available.

What are the choices?

Basically, there are FOUR types of pension. You will usually be entitled to one or more of these. Each is summarised below.

If you think you are entitled to one or more of these pensions and you want to know more about them, write to the TUC and ask for the relevant Pensions Factsheet.

The basic state pension

If you earn more than £58.00 each week, you may qualify for the basic state pension. The state pension is paid for through National Insurance contributions. These are deducted from your wages by your employer.

To qualify for a full pension, you must have paid enough contributions for enough years. If you have not paid enough contributions, you may qualify for a reduced pension.

If you are a married woman who chooses to pay reduced National Insurance contributions, called the 'small stamp', you will not qualify for a pension in your own right. Instead, you will get a pension based on your husband's contributions.

The state pension is paid by the Government. Men can get their state pension from age 65. Women can currently get their state pension from age 60.

The state pension is currently worth £61.15 per week for a single pensioner and £97.75 a week for a pensioner couple. This is not enough to live on and that's why it is important you start thinking about pensions early on.

Occupational pensions

You may have a pension that comes with your job. This is called an occupational pension. This is a scheme backed by your employer who will pay towards the benefits it will give you. You will also usually be required to pay towards the scheme.

An occupational pension is the best bet for most people. A good occupational pension scheme will give you: a pension related to how much you earn when you retire; a tax-free lump sum; benefits for your dependants when you die – either once you've retired or while you are still working; a lump sum benefit when you die; and benefits if you are forced to retire early, e.g. because of ill-health.

Because these benefits are related to how much you earn, they are guaranteed. Once they have been earned, they cannot be taken away.

How much pension you get will depend on how long you were in the scheme, how much you earned when you retired, and how quickly the pension builds up. So you can know in advance what your pension will be.

If your pension is linked to how much you earn like this, it is called a salary-related pension. This type of pension will generally provide the best benefits.

Not all occupational pensions are salary-related. Some work like a savings account: the pension at the end of the day will depend on how much you and your employer paid in, how well these contributions were invested and the rate of interest when you retire.

The benefits from these sorts of occupational pension schemes are not guaranteed. But the employer will usually pay something towards them.

State Earnings-related Pension Scheme

Usually, if you are not in a pension scheme that comes with your job, you will be in the State Earnings-related Pension Scheme (SERPS).

This is a pension scheme provided by the Government. The benefits it gives are linked to how much you earn over your

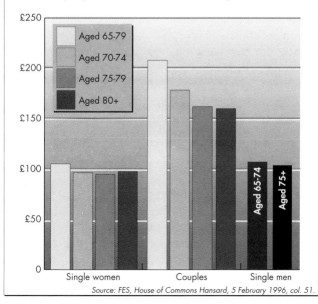

Weekly income by age and sex in 1993

The graph below shows that single men tend to have higher incomes than single women and that income levels tend to decrease with age. However, especially for single people, the differences are not great.

Aged 65-79
Aged 70-74
Aged 75-79
Aged 80+

Single women   Couples   Single men

Aged 65-74   Aged 75+

Source: FES, House of Commons Hansard, 5 February 1996, col. 51.

working life and how long you have been in the scheme.

You pay for SERPS through National Insurance contributions. These are deducted by your employer (who will also contribute) and are passed on to the Department of Social Security, the government department responsible for pensions.

But because of recent government changes to SERPS, it is unlikely to provide benefits which are as good as most occupational pension schemes.

In some cases, employers might provide an occupational pension on top of SERPS.

Personal pensions

Personal pensions are arrangements you can make yourself with banks, building societies or insurance companies.

Personal pensions are a form of private provision – they are not pensions which come with your job. Because of this, most employers will not contribute to them. This means you will have to pay in a lot to get back a decent-sized pension at the end.

Personal pensions work a bit like building-society accounts: you pay money in which is invested and which is used to buy a pension (called an annuity) from an insurance company when you retire.

The amount you can pay in depends on your age. It will be between 17.5% and 40% of your wages each year.

Despite all the publicity, personal pensions rarely give benefits anywhere near as good as occupational pensions.

The benefits you get will not be related to how much you earned when you retired. Instead, they will depend on how well your money was invested and on the state of the stock-market.

Personal pensions are a lot riskier than occupational schemes, even though in the short term they might be cheaper.

TUC advice

TUC advice says if you are in an occupational pension scheme, you should stay in.

If you have the chance to join an occupational pension scheme, you should do so. The earlier you start paying into a scheme, the bigger your pension will be at the end of the day.

© Trades Union Congress

Your pension

Information from the Association of Retired Persons (ARP / 050)

Pensions are a complex area, so only the rudiments are explained below. If you get into difficulty, ARP/050 will do our best to help.

State pension

To get a state pension you need to meet all of the following requirements:
1. You have reached state pension age (60 for a woman, 65 for a man).
2. You meet the National Insurance (NI) contribution conditions.
3. You claim it. (You should be sent claim form BR1 about 4 months before you reach pension age, but you must still fill it in to claim.)

The state pension has different components:

Basic pension
For 1996/1997 the full basic pension is £61.15 for a single person and £97.75 for a married couple.

To qualify for the full rate you need to have paid NI contributions

for 90% of your working life. A 'working life' is normally defined as 44 years for a woman and 49 years for a man. For the minimum basic pension – 25% of the full amount – you need 9-10 qualifying years. Years spent at school between 16 and 18 and for men aged between 60 and 65 are automatically credited.

Graduated pension
The Graduated Retirement Benefit applies to people employed between April 1961 and April 1975 when the scheme was in operation.

Additional pension
This is based on earnings since April 1978. It is the money paid under the State Earnings-Related Pension Scheme, or SERPS, and is only applicable if you have paid the full contributions to this scheme.

The calculations for additional pension are complicated and based on your level of contributions since 1978.

The amount of pension you receive could also be affected by whether you have a dependent spouse – in which case you may be able to get up to £36.60 extra. In effect the difference between a single person and that of a married couple. Other factors that could affect your pension are: receipt of Incapacity Benefit Age Addition before reaching state pension age and being aged over 80.

How much will you get?

This will very much depend on your employment history. You can get a pension forecast – providing you are more than 4 months away from state pension age – which will tell you the amount to expect. Form BR19 from your local Benefits Agency (Social Security) office explains how to do this.

Did you know?

- the real value of the state pension has declined since 1980 when it was linked to the increase in prices. Previously it was linked to the increase in prices or average earnings, whichever was the higher

- if you defer receiving your state pension by up to 5 years, you can increase the amount you get
- you can work and receive a state pension based on your own contributions
- if you are a married woman over 60 and you have not been employed, you may be able to get a basic pension based on your husband's NI contributions. But you will need to wait until he is 65
- you may be able to make additional contributions if there are gaps in your NI payment record
- since 1978, married women can claim NI credits if they were not working because they had children of school age
- if you go into hospital for NHS treatment, your pension will be reduced after 6 weeks
- if you go to live abroad, your state pension will still be paid to you
- when pensions rates increase in the UK, you will only receive the new rate if you live in a country with which the UK has a special agreement (currently the European Union countries and 37 non-EU countries)
- all state pensions are subject to income tax at your marginal tax rate.

Further information

Benefits Agency free helpline: 0800 666 555

Your local Benefits Agency or Social Security office

Free Benefits Agency booklet NP46 *A Guide to Retirement Pensions*

Occupational pensions

In addition to the state pension, you may also derive income from an occupational pension scheme run by your employer.

You are legally entitled to information about your scheme such as the pension amounts and entitlements you have built up and the rights and choices you have in deciding how to use them to your best advantage. You should ask the manager of the scheme for this. If you also ask for a copy of the rules, you can check that what you're getting is correct.

Further information

If the organisation you worked for has gone out of business, or you have lost the necessary paperwork, then the Occupational Pensions Board may be able to help. Write to: Office of the Registrar, PO Box 1NN, Newcastle-upon Tyne NE99 1NN.

If you are concerned about your rights under either an occupational scheme or a personal pension, you can get free help from this independent voluntary organisation: Occupational Pensions Advisory Service, 11 Belgrave Road, London SW1V lRP Telephone 0171 233 8080.

Additional voluntary contributions

One way of boosting your retirement income is by making additional voluntary contributions to your pension fund in the years immediately prior to your retirement. This is a very attractive way of making additional provision as all contributions to your pension through AVCs are tax free so that in effect the Inland Revenue are paying between £24-£40 (dependent on your tax rate) of every £100 you invest. All occupational schemes are obliged by law to make an AVC facility available. The total of AVCs plus your standard pension contribution cannot exceed 15% of your total earnings but at present with many companies offering contribution holidays to members this can be a highly efficient investment. You cannot however

take a lump sum payment from the AVC portion of a pension fund.

If you are uncertain about whether the amount of your pension has been calculated correctly, ARP/050 may be able to help.

Personal pensions

You are not compelled to buy an annuity from the company whose scheme you have been paying into. In fact, shopping around could increase your pension payments considerably. Under rules introduced in 1994, you are now allowed to defer buying an annuity until you are 75. Instead, you can withdraw income from the fund at a rate 'broadly equivalent' to that provided by annuities. One advantage is that, if you die before purchasing an annuity, the rest of the pension is returned to your estate.

Your retirement benefits will be based on the value of your personal account that has built up. This value will depend on the amount of your contributions, the investment performance of the relevant funds and the date you retire. When you retire you are entitled to:

- a tax-free cash sum of up to 25% of the fund
- a personal, taxable, income for life which can either be fixed or increased annually
- protection for your dependants, providing an income for them if you die first.

If you have contributed to a pension plan that doesn't mature until you are 60 or 65, and if you wish to retire before that, you should still be able to benefit from your pension, although you will suffer some penalties. You can check current annuity rates in the national press or via Teletext.

You can take advice from an independent adviser in purchasing an annuity from your investment fund and a number of companies specialise in doing this. If you would like further information on this possibility we can provide a list of possible providers.

- The above is an extract from the ARP 050 *Membership handbook 1996-1997*. See page 39 for address details.

The retired population

The number of older people in the UK

The number of older people in the population has increased over the past decades, and is projected to increase in the future.

Table 1: UK population (millions)

Year	1961	1981	1991	2001	2021
65-79	5.2	6.9	6.9	6.8	8.9
80+	1.0	1.6	2.1	2.6	3.2
Total 65+	6.2	8.5	9.0	9.4	12.1
Total pop.	52.8	56.4	57.8	59.8	62.1

Source: *Social Trends 25*, 1995, table 1.4

The ageing population

Despite the increase in the total number of older people, the overall percentage of people over 65 is projected to remain constant for some time at around 15-16% of the total population. As the above figures show, the number of people aged between 65 and 79 is actually projected to fall slightly in the next 10 years.

However, the section of the population which is increasing, both in actual size and in relation to the total population, is that of people over 80. The proportion of people in this age group is projected to increase from 1.9% in 1961 to 4.3% in 2001. Thus, even though the proportion of older people (65+) in the population is remaining more or less constant, an increasing number in this group will be very elderly. This could have a significant impact on such issues as the provision of support services in the community.

Table 2: Percentage of population aged 65-79 and 80+

Year	1961	1981	1991	2001	2021
65-79	9.8	12.2	12.0	11.4	14.3
80+	1.9	2.8	3.7	4.3	5.1
Total 65+	11.7	15.0	15.7	15.7	19.4

Source: *Social Trends 25*, 1995, table 1.4

Pensionable age

In 1994, there were 10.6 million people of pensionable age in the UK (Regional Trends 31, 1996, table 15.1). This represents 18.2% of the total population of the UK. The total for just Great Britain, as shown in the 1991 Census, is 10.3 million, 18.7% of the population as a whole. Pensionable age at present is 60 for women and 65 for men. It has been argued that this difference leads to discrimination (against both women and men, in different circumstances). The Government proposes to equalise the state pension age for men and women at 65, although this change is not intended to happen until 2010.

Life expectancy

In 1996, life expectancy at birth in the UK is expected to be 74.4 years for men and 79.7 years for women (Social Trends 26, 1996, table 7.3). Life expectancy increases with age: in England, a man aged 60 can expect to live a further 17.8 years to 77.8 and a woman aged 60 a further 22.1 years to 82.1 (Health and Personal Social Services Statistics 1995, table 3.3).

Life expectancy in the UK has increased steadily throughout this century. In 1931, life expectancy at birth was 58.4 (men) and 62.4 (women), and in 1961, 67.9 and 73.8 years respectively.

Gender structure

Women's higher life expectancy is demonstrated clearly in the male/female divide in the older population. In 1993, men formed 49% of the population of the UK as a whole, but only 30% of the over-eighties.

Table 3: Gender structure of the older population

	65-79	80+	all ages
Men	44%	30%	49%
Women	56%	70%	51%

Source: *Social Trends 25*, 1995, table 1.4

Retired households

One-third (32%) of all households in Great Britain are headed by a person aged 60 or over. Moreover, one in six (16%) of all households in Great Britain consist of one person aged 60+ living along (General Household Survey 1994, table 2.4).

What kind of households do older people live in?

The vast majority of people over pensionable age live in private (that is, non-institutional) housing. Only approximately 5% of people in this age group live in a residential or nursing home.

Of those living in private housing, more than a third (39%) live on their own. Just over half live with their partner: 46% just with their partner and 6% with their partner and other people. 7% live with relatives, such as children and siblings, and just 2% live with non-relatives (General Household Survey 1994, People aged 65 and over, table 6.3).

Over three-quarters of the elderly population therefore live either on their own or just with their partner in private housing. This demonstrates that, contrary to stereotype, most older people live independent lives in the community.   © *Help the Aged*

Thinking about early retirement?

Information from the Trades Union Congress

More and more people are retiring before they reach normal retirement age.

Sometimes this is out of choice, but often it is not: early retirement has, in some cases, become another word for redundancy.

This article tells you
- what early retirement is;
- when you can take early retirement;
- the circumstances in which you can retire early;
- the pension you will get; and
- about ill-health early retirement.

Finally, it sets out negotiating objectives for union representatives.

What is early retirement?

Early retirement is when you retire earlier than the age people normally retire at in your job. This is called the normal retirement age.

This will be the age that is set out in your contract of employment. It is the age to which you are normally expected to work.

When can you take early retirement?

If you have a pension that comes with your job: for men, the earliest date you can take early retirement (other then because of ill-health) and get a pension straight away is from age 50.

For women, the earliest date is also 50, providing that you would normally be expected to work until age 60. You may have an earlier retirement age, depending on when you joined the scheme.

This is the earliest the Inland Revenue will allow you to retire and get a pension.

Your occupational pension scheme may have its own rules on early retirement. For example, it

might say that you can retire from age 55 as long as you've been in the scheme for 20 years or more. So, before you can take early retirement, you should make sure you qualify. Ask your union rep, your member trustee, or your scheme manager.

If you are in a personal pension, the earliest you can take your pension is also from age 50. This is the same for women and men.

Why retire early?

People take early retirement for a number of reasons.

Many people choose to retire early. Even if the rules of the scheme allow this you may still need the permission of the employer. But more and more people are finding that employers are using pension schemes as a way of paying for redundancies – especially for older workers.

This could be called voluntary early retirement. But if the employer doesn't get enough people to retire voluntarily, early retirement can become compulsory. This is dealt with in more detail in the Factsheet on Redundancy and Pensions. People can also retire early on the grounds of ill-health. This is dealt with later in this article.

How much pension will you get?

To get a full pension, you will usually have to have been in a scheme for 40 years. So, if you are retiring early you will not have paid into the scheme for the full length of time and the pension has to be paid out for longer. The result will be that the pension you get will be smaller than if you had worked until normal retirement age. The pension you will get will depend on the type of scheme you are a member of.

If you are in an occupational pension scheme giving benefits based on your earnings, your pension will be based on the number of years you were in the scheme and how much you earned at the time you left.

When you leave the scheme, you are likely to find that your pension will be reduced by a certain percentage for each year or month that you take the pension before normal retirement age. For example, your benefits might be reduced by 0.5% for every month that you take the pension early. So, if you retire 2 years (24 months) early you will lose 12% in pension. This could mean a significant cut in the amount of pension you'll get.

If you're in an occupational scheme not based on how much you earn, or if you are in a personal pension, the amount you'll get depends on how much you and your employer have paid into the scheme.

The money paid in will be used to buy a pension (called an annuity) from an insurance company. If you retire early, your personal pension will be paid for longer than if you retired at normal retirement age. The same amount of money has to go further and so the pension paid to you will be reduced. Whichever type of scheme you're in, get an estimate of how much your early retirement pension will be.

Ask your union rep or your scheme manager. If you have a personal pension ask the company that sold you the pension.

Think very carefully about whether you can afford to take early retirement – you will be retiring on a smaller pension. It will be the pension you will get for life.

Ill-health early retirement

If you are not fit enough to work, you may be allowed to retire early on ill-health. If you have an occupational pension, you can retire on ill-health at any age and get an immediate pension. However, you must be said to be unfit to do your work. Your own scheme will have its own rules on what this means for you.

Usually, ill-health early retirement benefits are higher than other early-retirement benefits. This is because the pension may be based on the final pension you could have received if you had worked until your normal retirement age. But it will still be based on your earnings at the time of your actual retirement.

If you are in a scheme that is not related to your earnings, you can still retire on ill-health, but your pension will depend on how much has been paid into the scheme.

You may find it difficult to get life assurance cover if you retire because of ill-health. So make sure you are still covered by your employer's life assurance scheme.

The state pension

The state pension can only be paid from age 60 (women) and age 65 (men). It cannot be paid early.

If you do retire early, you may be entitled to other social security benefits, such as Income Support or Invalidity Benefit. Ask at your local Benefits Office.

You will also need to 'sign on' to get credits for your state pension so it continues to build up.

Checklist for negotiators

If your members are thinking about early retirement, here are some negotiating points to think about:

- make sure you discuss it with them;
- ensure the member knows the pension they'll end up with – this can often be a lot smaller than they thought;
- if pensions are reduced for early payment, try to abolish these reductions;
- ill-health pensions should take account of the service the member could have completed;
- people who retire early should still be covered by employers' life assurance policies;
- early retirements due to redundancies should take account of service members could have completed.

© Trade Union Congress

Nobody called

Michael Simmons reports on our shared responsibility for the old living and dying alone in our isolated society

John Sheppard died five years ago this month, not long after his 69th birthday. In fact, he had already been dead for some three and a half years when a couple of workmen, trying to trace a water leak, forced an entry into his one-bedroomed north London flat and found what remained of his decomposed body. The coroner criticised the local council where he had lived for 'most extraordinary complacency' in dealing with his affairs.

Every week of the year between 300 and 500 British pensioners, having lived a lonely and isolated existence, die alone, unnoticed and unattended in their own homes. Often, according to estimates from the concerned charities, they have been physically or mentally ill. Their deaths no longer make headlines and it is often weeks before local residents take notice. Help the Aged keeps a file of case-studies.

George Gaunt died last September. He was only 58, the popular chairman of the working men's club in the County Durham village where he lived. Neighbours, workmates and club members all thought he was on holiday when they didn't see him for several weeks. In fact, he had been suffering from gout and when the police broke in had been dead on the floor of his home for five weeks.

When Ian Pattison of Edinburgh died, also last September, it was the smell emanating from his front door and the swarms of flies which had suddenly converged on his home that drew attention. It was known that he had been in hospital and treated for depression but when a council worker forced entry into his flat, Pattison had already been dead for at least nine months. He had apparently hanged himself at the new year.

Charities say nearly half of all the over-65s (almost one in 12 of the population) and almost two-thirds of women over 75 now live alone.

Many are in good health and enjoy life but for others community care programmes, designed to encourage independent living, seem to have complicated an already difficult situation. Lines of responsibility are vague. At least some of the hundreds who will die this week will have fallen through the gaps which seem to be growing between health and social workers – or between them and some other ostensible service provider. 'Who is looking after these people?' asks the overstretched and under-resourced social worker. 'A lot of departments have them on their books and a lot of people throw up their hands in horror at the situation – but still these people go unvisited.'

Frequently, after a lonely death, fingers are pointed – for the wrong reasons – at the local council. The legal position is such that a local authority has to move carefully if it wants to know if a person in their own home needs help, or is unwell – or even dead. It has no general duty to seek out those at risk but it can be legally liable for 'nuisance' if a

---

Every week of the year between 300 and 500 British pensioners, having lived a lonely and isolated existence, die alone, unnoticed and unattended in their own homes

---

decomposing body, rotting food, poor sanitation or 'seepage of body fluids' gives rise to a nuisance.

And what of more traditional and informal community networks that seem to have broken down? Where the population density is more than a handful to the acre, you will hear that the neighbours don't 'look in' the way they used to do, that nobody sees to the rent and nobody notices if the milk starts piling up on the step. A certain security has also gone. Housing managers know what old people about to be rehoused crave

most, to be safe walking their own neighbourhood. They used not to keep their front doors locked.

Although most older people say they are well enough to look after themselves, many depend on that secret army of carers – between five and seven million, looking after someone over 65. But one in five is over 65 themselves, two out of every three say their own health is suffering, while nearly half have financial difficulties.

Wally Harbert at Help the Aged, a former social services director, has closely studied the situation of the isolated elderly and, at the local council's request, led an inquiry into John Sheppard's death. In a recent paper for the Policy Studies Institute, he concludes that 'the problems surrounding lonely deaths go to the heart of a contemporary, mobile and ageing society.' He calls for a partnership between statutory and voluntary services to develop strategies that will reduce isolation and bring in 'the whole community.'

Britain 'facing crisis' over care of the elderly

Britain is facing a major care crisis because people are ignoring their future needs and those of their relatives, according to a survey published yesterday.

Many believe they will be provided for in later years. But the Carers National Association (CNA) fears they may be left in the lurch by 'small changes carried out by stealth'.

A poll commissioned by the charity shows only 4 in 10 people have given thought to who would care for them if they could no longer manage on their own.

Three out of four admit they have made no financial provision. And while most families are willing to care for their relatives, 6 out of 10 expect to receive some cash help from the state.

Less than half (47 per cent) say they would be willing to make compulsory extra payments towards the cost of caring for the frail or disabled.

One in four said he or she would be willing to make some voluntary payments, while the rest did not want to make any extra contribution.

The statistics, prepared for the CNA by Boots the Chemist, are based on an NOP poll of 902 non-carers.

It showed that women (53 per cent) are more likely than men (38 per cent) to have thought about what they would do if a relative needed care – and were more prepared to carry out tasks.

Nine out of 10 men and women would be prepared to do the

shopping. However, 75 per cent of women would wash or bathe in their role as a carer against only 55 per cent of men.

The study follows the new Carers Act which took effect on 1 April and entitles carers to an assessment of their needs.

Jill Pitkeathley, chief executive of the CNA, said the survey highlighted the need for caring to be given a higher priority.

'People are not making provision for their future because they are acting on the premise that they will be provided for in old age.

'This is no longer the case. We must face the issue and be open about what we can and cannot afford.

'Otherwise we are heading for a serious crisis.'

Myth of the 'geriatric timebomb' is exploded

MPs back means-testing for nursing home benefits

By David Fletcher, Health Correspondent

Fears that the growing number of elderly needing care and the fewer younger people in work will swamp the tax and benefits system are a myth, according to a report by MPs published yesterday.

The parliamentary health committee said projections showed that demand for care in old age would rise but there would be no dramatic surge and the cost to the taxpayer would be affordable at least until 2031.

'The projections do not support claims that we face a "demographic timebomb", or at least not one that is likely to explode over the next two to three decades,' the report stated.

The all-party committee looked at a variety of measures to enable the elderly to be cared for in nursing or residential homes without imposing a crippling burden on the tax system or forcing them to sell their homes.

The report concludes that keeping the existing system – under which NHS care is free and social care is means-tested – is a 'major option in its own right'.

It is highly critical of the Government's proposal earlier this year for a partnership scheme intended to enable old people to pay for nursing home care without having to sell their houses.

'We would be worried by any suggestion that partnership schemes are "the answer" to the problems of long-term care funding,' it said.

'We deprecate the Government's failure to provide even rough-and-ready costings of its various options. Until such costings are provided, the taxpayer is in effect being invited to sign a blank cheque.'

Under the Government's partnership scheme, old people would be able to keep their home by taking out insurance to pay for a limited period of care in a nursing home – perhaps three years – with the state paying the fees thereafter.

Under existing arrangements the value of a person's home is taken into account in assessing their liability to pay fees and thousands have had to sell their homes to pay for care.

The committee backs a proposal by the Royal College of Nursing that nursing care should be provided free on the NHS while the accommodation costs of care homes would continue to be paid for through means-testing.

It said: 'The RCN's suggestion has the merit that it would tackle the most manifest unfairness in the present system – the way health care is currently defined to exclude nursing care in nursing homes. Many members of the public quite understandably find this definition baffling.'

It dismisses long-term care insurance as too expensive for more than a small minority of the population.

The value of a person's home is taken into account in assessing their liability to pay fees and thousands have had to sell their homes to pay for care

It condemns as 'flawed' suggestions that pensioners should take a smaller pension on retirement with a larger pension later on to pay for care in a home.

But it backs 'equity-release' schemes – under which old people can gain income by committing a proportion of the value of their home – provided they are properly regulated.

The committee concludes; 'Until such time as the Government divulges its own estimates of the likely cost of each option, including the likely costs of its preferred option of partnership schemes, it will not be possible to reach a final decision on the best way forward.

'Decisions on whether long-term care should be funded through general taxation or through insurance touch upon fundamental questions concerning the future of the welfare state and cannot be tackled in relation to long-term care in isolation.'

Tessa Jowell, shadow health minister, said that the report amounted to a 'stern reprimand' for the Government for its 'irresponsible scaremongering about spiralling costs of long-term care'.

Sally Greengross, director of Age Concern, said the manifest unfairness of the present system would be tackled if the NHS met all nursing care costs in old people's homes.

She said: 'Such a move would be heartily endorsed by Age Concern. We would have liked to have seen more clarification of where the boundaries lie between health and social care.

'This is at the heart of the issue for many older people.'

Value of home 'should fund care in old age'

By Nicholas Timmins,
Public Policy Editor

The Government should initiate a new-equity release scheme to allow elderly people to use part of the value of their home to cover their long-term care, a left-of-centre think-tank said yesterday.

For an average £60,000 home, a couple might have to give up about 45 per cent of its value – less if it was worth more, more if it was worth less – with a lower percentage for single people.

But the cash would provide an insurance which could guarantee cover against the cost of long-term care. The home would only be sold on death and a guaranteed proportion of the home's value would be passed on as an inheritance.

The call to create Peris – partial equity-release insurance schemes – came from the Institute of Public Policy Research, as it warned that the costs of long-term care, both in people's own homes and in residential and nursing homes, was set to escalate dramatically. Even allowing for economic growth, costs would more than double in real terms by 2031, taking about 5 per cent of national income, against 1.8 per cent now.

The present system of means-tested care, which this year is expected to see 40,000 people having to sell their homes, is inequitable, demeaning for people who have always been financially independent and discourages savings, the report says.

Longer-term options include creating a new pay-as-you-go social insurance, which would be expensive; building a funded social insurance which would take 30 years to mature;

opting for partial cover – running collective insurance for care costs but not 'hotel' costs of long-term care; or developing private/public partnership schemes.

> **For an average £60,000 home, a couple might have to give up about 45 per cent of its value – less if it was worth more, more if it was worth less**

The last of these is being actively considered by ministers, who have promised a White Paper on funding long-term care. Where individuals cover themselves through insurance for a fixed sum of care, the state would add that to the £16,000 of assets which individuals are able to keep when they fall back on means-tested care.

Peris could help with that, according to the author of the report, Ed Richards, a consultant with London Economics, and former adviser to Gordon Brown, the shadow Chancellor.

Today, about 40 per cent of those who retire own their own homes, a figure likely to reach 65 per cent in 20 years' time.

Creating Peris – something the financial services industry is unlikely to do without government assistance – could take advantage of that, reducing public spending but without forcing individuals to sell their homes during their lifetime.

'At the moment, it is an all-or-nothing situation,' Mr Richards said. Individuals either had to invest in private long-term care insurance during their working life, which was incredibly expensive, or take the risk of almost all their assets being means-tested away. Creating Peris would provide something in between – allowing many individuals to pre-serve at least some of their assets for inheritance while protecting themselves, either completely or partially, from falling back on to means-tested care.

● *Paying for Long-Term Care*; IPPR, 30-32 Southampton Street, London WC2E 7RA; £9.95

Paying for residential care

Government's reward for those years of scrimping to buy your own homes

The trauma of being forced to sell their homes to pay for residential or nursing home care is being faced by an increasing number of elderly people. So much for the vaunted 'property-owning democracy'.

Forced to respond to the growing scandal, the Government recently announced an upgrading of the minimum required assets, which includes property. When they amount to less than £10,000, they will not be required for the cost of care and anyone with £16,000 or less may qualify for some state aid. Above that, they must pay the fees in full.

Depending on nursing requirements, fees could be anything between £15,000 and £30,000 a year. It could, moreover, be argued that the cost of medical care should be borne by the NHS.

Greater demands

With the closing down of many geriatric wards, the old and frail have nowhere else to go.

Prudent people on comparatively low wages often scrimped and scraped to pay off home mortgages when their families were young. Later, when council houses were being sold off and few were being built, there was an acute shortage of houses to rent.

Social conditions changed, too. People now live much longer and make more demands on incomes and benefits, which barely keep pace with the cost of living since the Government changed the rules for pensions which used to be based on average wages and now are adjusted to the cost of living.

Nor are future prospects bright, for compulsory early retirement results in lower pension pay-outs and the increasing use of part-time labour means no proper pension rights and fewer occupational pension schemes, a boon to many unable to subsist on the state pension.

In what has been described as 'a web of bureaucratic buck-passing' the Government now imposes strict limits on available resources and caps funding to local authorities on to whom they have devolved all responsibility for the care of the elderly.

Don't get old unless you are well-off

The fundholding scheme for GPs means that it is more profitable for them to devote their attention and time to younger, healthier patients, and pressure is often put on some of the elderly to enter residential homes if the costs of domiciliary care exceed that of residential.

The Government is now urging people to take out long-term care provision with a pound-for-pound deal with the private insurance sector. This is a godsend for insurance companies whose core business has collapsed but out of the question for most pensioners struggling to make ends meet.

When it was clear that local authorities could not afford to run homes directly the owners of small hotels, boarding houses, and even country mansions, jumped on the lucrative bandwagon. They now find the going harder as local authorities are able to strike stiffer bargains over fees, especially where there is over-provision of residential care in particular localities.

People are also being moved out of inner-city areas, where there is a lack of provision, where they have always lived and where their families still live, to remote seaside resorts.

Although many care-home owners try to do a good job under considerable difficulties, others are less conscientious and pay their staff appallingly low wages.

The standard of inspection also varies, and some homes are described as 'unhappy'. The Joseph Rowntree Foundation has estimated that about 10 per cent give inspectors 'cause for acute concern'.

The under-resourcing of the social services also makes monitoring more difficult.

Sally Greengross, director-general of Age Concern England, is worried that not enough people know the system is changing and that very little is being done by the Government to keep people informed.

She exhorts the elderly to fight for their rights, collectively and individually. 'Ask your care-home owner for more information and your local authority, the Benefits Agency and the local Age Concern group.

'Take a little time to check – it could save money,' she said. Citizens Advice Bureaux and charities like the Alzheimer's Disease Society and Help the Aged are eager to help the many thousands who are not claiming housing benefit or council tax allowance to which they are entitled.

The economics of the marketplace, with its complete dependence on supply and demand, has taken over and, in capitalist jargon, it is necessary to 'investigate the market'.

As Will Hutton, editor of *The Guardian*, has warned: 'The message in contemporary Britain could hardly be more stark: don't get old unless you are well-off. Death, like life, has been privatised.'

© British Pensioner, British Pensioners' and Trade Union Action Association Summer, 1996

Paying for nursing homes

Some answers to questions about paying for nursing care in old age

As controversy continues over the Government's proposals to make it easier for the elderly to meet nursing home fees, Teresa Hunter offers a guide to plans less radical than they seem.

Why are the elderly and their families suddenly being asked to pay for health care?

They aren't – at least not medical care. But as people live longer and the quality of their lives deteriorates, more will need to be looked after in nursing homes. More than 500,000 people are cared for in homes, and this will rise to 1.3 million by 2050.

How much does a nursing home cost?

Between £10,000 and £30,000 a year depending on location and the level of care. Most patients with severe disabilities will be charged around £20,000 annually.

What if you don't have enough money? Surely the state will pay?

If you are worth more than £16,000 – and that includes your home – forget about state support. The elderly with savings of between £10,000 and £16,000 may qualify for a small amount of help. Even below that level, complicated income calculations, including all pensions and earnings from shares and building society accounts, may still disqualify you.

But surely they can't sell the roof over my partner's head or take my pension?

The house is protected if a spouse, or a retired or disabled relative, lives there. Similarly, half an occupational pension may be disregarded from the income calculations if needed to maintain a spouse. Limited protection of the house and other savings may be offered under the Government's proposals.

So the Government has decided to pay for our nursing care and we can keep our homes after all?

Not quite – in fact not at all. Health Secretary Stephen Dorrell has made four proposals – two based on existing long-term care insurance and the others on pension and home income plan arrangements – which do little more than flag up existing options.

The Government is proposing, however, to allow people who buy insurance to 'ring-fence' assets such as their savings and their house. They can shelter assets equivalent to what an insurer pays out over four years plus an additional £15,000. Alternatively, they can benefit from a £1.50 disregard for every £1 insurance cover.

I'm completely lost and what does all this cost anyway?

Here's an example. A 40-year-old woman could today buy £10,000 worth of nursing care each year she needed it for a lump sum of £14,783 – or a monthly premium of £43.90.

Mr Dorrell proposed that for each £10,000 the insurer pays out, £15,000 of her assets are ring-fenced.

Alternatively, after four years of paying her own way, she can shelter £15,000 of her wealth plus another sum equivalent to her insurance claims.

Isn't this expensive?

Yes it is, particularly when you all but double these costs to cover a spouse. And of course neither of them may need it at all as only one in five people go into homes. Or they may hate their offspring and not give a damn about cascading their wealth down on them.

But are these insurance policies a good idea?

All policies have exclusions and can be difficult to claim on. Insurance can never provide a fail-safe safety-net. People will have to pass incapacity tests, and there are dangers that those in most need will be sold the wrong kind of cover. Ever heard of the long-term care scandal? You will have soon.

What about the other options?

The Government also suggested allowing people to take a lower pension when they first retire to pay for long-term care later. The problem is most pensioners are already poverty-stricken.

Finally, home income plans allow people to take out a loan on their home to buy a regular income through an annuity – another kind of insurance. But no one has yet devised an annuity which could meet interest payments and nursing home fees.

Furthermore, hundreds of elderly have already faced repossession because of home income plans which went wrong. Either way you could end up losing your home.

Meeting the cost of continuing care

Public views and perceptions

A Joseph Rowntree Foundation Inquiry is currently considering options for financing continuing care for older people. A qualitative study among people of all ages, undertaken for the Inquiry by Rebecca Diba of Social and Community Planning Research, reveals how the public view the key issues involved. She found:

- There was widespread criticism of the current system of funding long-term care for older people. The means-testing of payment for residential care was the focus of particular complaint.

- The existence of a National Health Service, and the obligation to pay tax and National Insurance, had led people to expect that care for older people would be free at the point of delivery. The state's failure to fulfil this expectation strongly influenced people's views about future funding.

- People believed that revenue from supposedly dedicated contributions such as National Insurance has not been used for its intended purpose. This undermined their faith in a state-led system for funding long-term care.

- Any new system of tax or social insurance for long-term care must meet some key standards to be acceptable. People wanted assurance that any revenue collected would be dedicated to a stated purpose, would be properly invested and would guarantee the provision of a specified level of care.

- People see a role for private insurance in the future. Some envisage that it may be the only option for the younger generation; others hope that it will work alongside state funding, with the state paying for a minimum level of care and private insurance being used to 'top up' care to a higher standard.

- There was a view that the family should not be obliged to care for elderly relatives, and that those who are carers should be compensated for their time.

Introduction

As the number of people needing long-term care rises and the costs of providing care increase, the question of how the costs of continuing care will be met in the future becomes ever more pressing. In 1995 the Joseph Rowntree Foundation set up an Inquiry to investigate this issue. As part of their review, the Inquiry group required some understanding of the general public's attitudes towards the funding of long-term care of older people. The aim of this study was to explore public views about the current state funding system and to examine where responsibility for funding long-term care is felt to lie and how it should be paid for in the future.

At the time of the research, state funding of long-term care varied according to the circumstances of the individual and the type of care they required. State funding of care in nursing or residential homes was means-tested such that if a person's capital exceeded £8,000 they were no longer eligible for financial support from the state (in the 1995 autumn budget this was raised to

£16,000). Domiciliary care services supplied by local authorities were also subject to a means test.

Study participants' current experience of, or involvement in, the long-term care of older people was very varied. At one end of the spectrum there were people, more often younger respondents, who had no personal experience of long-term care. At the other end of the spectrum, some of the older respondents needed care themselves and the subject was therefore very close to their hearts.

Although some respondents had no experience of long-term care, most had a degree of awareness of how it was currently paid for in the UK. Participants' thoughts on funding long-term care were heavily influenced by their attitudes towards the existing state system of care provision. Thus, their views on the funding debate tended to mirror what they saw as problematic within the current system.

Injustices of the state funding system

'They will take it all away from you, if you've been careful during your life, if you bought your house, if you've saved, if you've invested your money you go into a residential home and you pay . . . there are people I have known . . . who throughout their life have spent what they have earned, they've lived for the day . . . now why in effect should I subsidise them, when my husband and I both worked hard all our lives? We were both extremely careful and we both thought we were going to have a little to spare in our old age.' (Rose, age 72)

The current system of funding the long-term care of older people was generally regarded as being unjust in certain key respects:

- People felt that they had been given a false promise by the state that long-term care for older people would be provided free at the point of delivery.
- The means-testing system for residential and nursing home care was felt to be unfair because it meant that thrifty individuals who had been careful and saved their money would have to pay

towards their care, whilst the spendthrift would be eligible for state funding.

- The £8,000 threshold was thought to be far too low, particularly given that property as well as savings and investments were accounted for in the means test. The idea of being forced to sell their home to pay for care caused great distress amongst some people. This was partly because they had hoped to leave it to their children as their largest financial resource. For many it also represented an asset which they had worked hard to achieve.
- It was widely felt that nursing care for older patients should be provided free, within the services offered by the National Health Service. People were angry that such care was no longer free to all those who needed it.
- There was some objection to local authority charging for domiciliary care services.

Options for state funding

'It doesn't matter what you pay into, whether it's pensions, hospitals, road tax – it's all in the pot . . . so whether you pay £20 extra a week to put your mother or granny into a home, it still goes in the pot.' (Stewart, age 49)

The public's opinions of the existing system helped to shape their views on where they felt responsibility for financing long-term care in nursing and residential homes lay. The overwhelming view was that people should see some return from money they had paid into the state through National Insurance and taxes.

However, although it was felt that the state should take a greater responsibility for funding long-term care, the public voiced concern about the ability of the state to fund care in the future. People believed that revenue from supposedly dedicated contributions, such as National Insurance, had not been used for its intended purpose, but put 'into the pot' along with other government revenue. There was concern that revenue collected in the name of long-term care would follow the same path.

People also said that they would be reluctant to fund care if the injustices of the current system were not redressed. Thus, for people to willingly pay more into the state, funding of long-term care would have to be seen to be fair and just. There were different views on how a just funding system could be established:

Some people proposed a totally statutory system of long-term care. *'I think everybody's entitled to a basic [level of] good quality care . . . You could fall on hard times, you can't punish people and say you didn't pay in so you get the basic care and you've got lots of money so you have good care.'*

(Joan, age 56)

Others thought that the state should fund a basic level of care, leaving people with the choice of paying privately if they wanted a higher standard – a 'top-up' option. *'There should be a baseline [that] everybody's entitled to which is good . . . but when you get that level you've got a choice, then you can buy [a better standard of care], just like a hotel, you can get a basic hotel, you can get a five-star hotel.'* (Mark, age 27)

Some people took the view that individuals should make a contribution towards the 'hotel' costs in state-run homes by paying something towards the cost of accommodation, meals or domestic services. However, generally, there was strong objection to the proposal for residents in nursing and residential homes to pay the full hotel costs. People suspected that the hotel costs would amount to considerably more than the care costs and that they would be no better off than under the existing system.

A further suggestion was to retain the current system of state funding in essence, but to increase the means-test limit to a more realistic level, allowing people to retain a significant portion of their capital.

In any event, taxpayers wanted assurance that their tax or social insurance would be dedicated to long-term care, that revenue collected would be put into a separate fund and invested and that a good standard of care would be guaranteed.

People recognised that the need for long-term care would increase in the future because of greater longevity within the population and the lack of adequate resources to pay for the care of an enlarging elderly population. Even if a state funding system conformed to the principles outlined above, some people would still doubt whether the state could meet the increased demand for long-term care. Whilst the proportion of the population needing long-term care was increasing, the proportion of taxpayers in the population was thought to be decreasing. Some people suggested, therefore, that the younger generation in particular might have to start planning private means of paying for long-term care, through private insurance for example.

Options for private funding of care

'Eventually we'll probably be trained to think about paying for our old age . . . extra pension to pay for when you have to go into a home . . . I can certainly see . . . in the foreseeable future that younger people at a certain age bracket will be asked to consider it.'

(Bob, age 66)

Some people were opposed to any form of private funding. Others could see a role for it in certain circumstances. Some suggested that savings and investments could be used to make a contribution towards the cost of their keep in a residential or nursing home or to pay for domiciliary care. Although the idea of using housing equity to pay for care initially provoked strong objections, on reflection circumstances were identified when people would be more willing to sell their home to finance long-term care:

- to pay for 'top-up' care above basic state care
- to pay for sheltered accommodation.

Likewise, people could see a role for private insurance in the future, either for the younger generation, in place of state funding, or as well as state funding to pay for 'top-up' care.

Options for funding through the family

Under the existing system, unpaid carers, usually a person's relative and often a woman, provide the greatest proportion of care. There was considerable debate as to whether family members should be expected to care for their relatives. At one end of the scale, some people argued that relatives should care for their family 'out of love' for them, or through a sense of duty or moral obligation.

At the other extreme, it was felt that people should not feel obliged to look after a relative if they did not have a good relationship with them. Moreover, it was also said that people may lose respect for their older relatives if traditional caring and supporting roles were reversed.

'A lot of people go back to living with [their] parents again. You . . . leave [home] when you're 18 to 20 or whatever . . . you've developed into a totally different person than when you were 18 and to try and live as a family again and look after them, you're not going to get on . . . you're not being looked after, you're not having your breakfast made by Mum, you're making her breakfast.'

(Richard, age 24)

People identified circumstances which would affect willingness to care for a relative, which included:

- the geographical distance between the carer and their relative
- the amount of space in the carer's home
- the level of work commitments
- whether the carer has young children at home
- the health of the carer.

An individual's willingness to care was said to depend on the type of care involved and the closeness of the relative who needed care. Moreover, it was also said that the views of the person needing care should be considered. It was felt that some individuals would not want to be looked after by their relatives, for fear either of losing their independence or of being a burden on their family.

There were mixed views on whether the family should be compensated for caring for relatives. Some people disputed the idea of compensation, and felt that people should care for relatives out of love or a sense of obligation. However, it was more often said that there should be a payment scheme for people caring for relatives. In some people's view, compensation should be available in all situations. Others felt that compensation should be awarded in certain circumstances. For example, if a person was forced to give up or cut back on their work, they should be reimbursed by the state for loss of earnings.

The suggestion that the family should pay for a relative's care was put to respondents, although it was not an issue that was mentioned spontaneously. People tended to think in terms of children whose parents needed care. It was thought that many people would not be able to afford to meet the costs of care and, having paid National Insurance and tax, people should be entitled to free care from the state. However, there were some people who felt that children should be expected at least to contribute towards the costs of their parents' care if they did not want to look after them.

Further information

The above is a summary from a report, *Meeting the costs of continuing care: Public views and perceptions*, published for the Joseph Rowntree Foundation by York Publishing Services, available from: York Publishing Services Ltd, 64 Hallfield Road, Layerthorpe, York YO3 7XQ Tel: 01904 430033, (ISBN 1 899987 15 0, price £11.00 plus £1.00 p+p).

© Joseph Rowntree Foundation
April, 1996

Créche takes grannies back to childhood

Britain's first ever 'granny créche,' where people can leave elderly relatives, is due to open in Oxford this summer.

Employees of the Radcliffe Hospital NHS Trust can leave grandparents in a 'stimulating environment' with art classes, cookery, memory strategies and indoor hockey. There will also be outings to Blenheim Palace, shopping centres and pubs. The trust is running a pilot scheme with 20 places in an adapted day unit staffed by nurses and occupational therapists.

When the idea was first suggested by the occupational department it was 'greeted with delight' by carers and their relatives, said Mike Fleming, the director of personnel. 'Besides the advantage of proximity [to each other] they will be in a hospital with nursing care and no worries about special feeds or dressings,' he said.

The pilot scheme, emphasising 'dignity and quality of life', is free and will run from 8.30am to 5.30pm, Monday to Friday, but it is hoped it will be extended to 8am to 8pm, seven days a week. If it is made permanent, fees of about £2 an hour will be charged.

Lynch Mason, the occupational therapy services manager, said there would be no lower age limit for the service. It will be open for 'anyone who feels comfortable and wants to go'. Activities will be tailored to individuals: 'We'll cater for people's interests whether that is art, sculpture, adult literacy or doing the crossword.

'Cookery groups are extremely popular and the elderly person could take a meal home in the evening so they feel they are contributing something to the family,' added Miss Mason.

At the moment there are almost

By Glenda Cooper

11 million people of pensionable age in Britain. That figure is expected to rise to almost 17 million within the next 35 years.

Terry Philpot, editor of *Community Care* magazine, said: 'Any initiative which provides high standards of care for elderly people and takes the pressure off carers should be welcomed. We are ill-prepared for the coming population explosion among elderly people.'

Charities representing pensioners expressed reservations. A spokeswoman for Help The Aged said: 'We welcome initiatives to set up "granny créches" but they must be active places providing a stimulating environment, not just dumping grounds for elderly relatives.'

© *The Independent*
May, 1996

Slow: Fun-loving OAPs ahead

There are many signs of ageing – and not all to do with being frail and lacking fun.

The residents of one old folks' home were so unhappy with the traditional traffic warning depicting a stooped couple with a walking stick that they decided to create their own.

The results show they haven't one foot anywhere near the grave. The four new signs – of elderly people on a skateboard, a unicycle, a pogo-stick and a wheelchair doing 'wheelies' – now adorn the mile-long private road to the home called Ysguborwen at Aberdare, Mid Glamorgan.

Home administrator Jacqui Coombes said: 'Our old folk lead very active lives and are not keen on the government signs. They show a doddery old couple which is not in keeping with the young-at-heart outlook of our residents. We are proud to be a very active home.'

The 70 residents at Ysguborwen go on coach trips to pubs and concerts and outings on canal barges. They also work out with weights in the home's gym. Resident Eddie Tovey, 83, said: 'We are not an ordinary old folks' home. We keep fit and active and these signs are great.'

© *The Daily Mail*
August, 1996

Greying population stays in the pink

By Philip Cohen,
San Francisco

Elderly people are growing healthier, happier and more independent, say American scientists. The results of a 14-year study to be announced later this month reveal that the diseases associated with old age are afflicting fewer and fewer people, and, when they do strike, it is much later in life. The findings suggest that the greying of the world's population may prove less of a financial burden than expected.

Since 1982, the National Long-Term Care Survey has gathered data on the health and lifestyles of more than 20,000 men and women over 65. Researchers now analysing the results of data gathered in 1994 say arthritis, high blood pressure and circulation problems – the major medical complaints in this age group – are troubling a smaller proportion every year. And the data confirm that the rate at which these diseases are declining continues to accelerate. Other diseases of old age – dementia, stroke, arteriosclerosis and emphysema – are also troubling fewer and fewer people.

'It really raises the question of what should be considered normal ageing,' says Kenneth Manton, a demographer from Duke University in Carolina. He says the problems doctors accepted as normal in a 65-year-old in 1982 are often not appearing until people are 70 or 75.

Clearly, certain diseases are beating a retreat in the face of medical advances. But more subtle factors are probably playing a part too. Improvements in childhood nutrition in the first quarter of the century, for example, gave today's elderly people a better start in life than their predecessors.

On the downside, the data also reveal failures in public health that have caused surges in some illnesses. An increase in some cancers and the steady creep of bronchitis may reflect changing smoking habits and poorer air quality, say the researchers. 'These may be subtle influences,' says Manton. 'But our subjects have been exposed to worse and worse pollution for over 60 years. It's not surprising we see some effect.'

One interesting correlation Manton uncovered is that better-educated people are likely to live longer. For example, 65-year-old women with fewer than eight years of schooling are expected on average to live to 82. Those who continued their education live an extra seven years. Although some of this can be attributed to a higher income, Manton believes it is mainly because educated people seek more medical attention.

The survey also assessed how independent people over 65 were, and again found a striking tend. Almost 80 per cent of those in the 1994 survey could complete everyday activities ranging from eating and dressing unaided to complex tasks such as cooking and managing their finances. That represents a significant drop in the number of disabled old people in the population.

If the trends apparent in the US 14 years ago had continued, researchers calculate there would be an additional 1 million disabled elderly people in today's population. According to Manton, slowing the trend has saved the US Government's Medicare system more than $200 billion.

Part of the improved independence of elderly people stems from an explosion in the use of simple home medical aids. For instance, the use of raised toilet seats more than doubled since the start of the study, and the use of bath seats grew by more than 50 per cent.

Increased self-reliance can bring some health benefits, according to a report from the MacArthur Foundation's research group on successful ageing. The group found that in elderly people a sense of independence and control over one's life, as well as some physical activity, were going predictors of who would stay healthy in old age.

Maintaining a level of daily activity may help mental functioning, says Carl Cotman, a neuroscientist at the University of California at Irvine. He found that rats that exercise on a treadmill have raised levels of brain-derived neurotrophic factor coursing through their brains. Cotman believes this hormone, which keeps neurons functioning, may prevent the brains of active humans from deteriorating.

As part of the same study, Teresa Seeman, a social epidemiologist at the University of Southern California in Los Angeles, found a connection between self-esteem and stress in people over 70. In laboratory simulations of challenging activities such as driving, those who felt in control of their lives pumped out lower levels of stress hormones such as cortisol. Chronically high levels of these hormones have been linked to heart disease.

But independence can have drawbacks. Seeman found that elderly people who felt emotionally isolated maintained higher levels of stress hormones even when asleep. The research suggests that older people fare best when they feel independent but know they can get help when they need it.

Like much research into ageing, these results support common sense, says Seeman. They also show that we may be underestimating the impact of these simple factors. 'The sort of thing that your grandmother always told you turns out to be right on target,' she says.

Laughter really is the best medicine

By Helen Carroll

If you want to reach a ripe old age, put a smile on your face, say researchers. Scientists have discovered that a group of life-enhancing chemicals are triggered when we burst into laughter.

These powerful hormones can boost the immune system, helping to ward off colds and flu, and might even help fight cancer.

Arthur Stone, a professor of psychoneural immunology at the State University of New York, has published a paper outlining the most conclusive evidence yet of a link between laughter and the levels of immunoglobulin A, an antibody found in the mucus which lines the nose.

The professor asked 72 men to fill in a form every evening for 12 weeks describing how good their day had been. Each of the participants also gave a daily mucus sample.

Professor Stone said: 'On days when they had laughed a lot there was more antibody and on bad days there was much less.

'Those people who had less antibodies were more prone to colds and other infections.'

Immunoglobulin A helps fight illness by identifying bacteria, viruses and potential tumour cells, which are then destroyed by white blood cells.

An average six-year-old laughs 300 times a day but by adulthood the daily tally has slumped to 47. Some sad individuals struggle to reach six chuckles a day

Perhaps surprisingly, the research also shows that smoking and drinking can boost levels of these hormones.

Chocolate, normally said to be bad for the health because of its high cholesterol and calorie count, is also one of the biggest triggers.

Veteran comedian Bernard Manning, 66, said laughter was a medicine which some people did not get enough of.

'I've always been a laugher and I've never seen the inside of a hospital,' he added.

Unfortunately, the tendency to laugh decreases with age.

An average six-year-old laughs 300 times a day but by adulthood the daily tally has slumped to 47. Some sad individuals struggle to reach six chuckles a day.

Women laugh more than men, particularly when they are talking.

Family care 'lacking for elderly blacks and Asians'

Elderly people in black and Asian communities may be less able to rely for support on their families than is commonly supposed, a report today warns.

Although only 3 per cent of the ethnic minority population is over 65, many younger black and Asian people may in future need community care, researchers say.

Having interviewed almost 100 pensioners from ethnic minority groups, the researchers conclude there is conflicting evidence as to whether such people's care needs are met by their families.

Asian people may present a particular challenge, the report says. 'Not wanting to place too much of a burden on their family was a common response, which sits uneasily with suggestions that the extended family successfully meets the needs of many older Asian people.'

The report, by Counsel and Care, an elderly care charity, is based on the circumstances and views of 96 elderly people at day centres, meeting places, and in sheltered housing schemes in London, Leicester, Birmingham and Wolverhampton.

It says there is an urgent need to make care services more sensitive to the requirements of older ethnic minority people – even though, paradoxically, many residential and nursing homes are run by Asians.

One Nigerian Muslim man told the researchers he could not contemplate residential care because he knew dietary arrangements would be unacceptable. One Hindu woman said: 'I know of people who have been fed beef.'

Generally, those interviewed were wary of making demands upon formal welfare systems because of feared discrimination and because of being seen as scrounging.

By David Brindle, Social Services Correspondent

Les Bright, the charity's deputy general manager, said one of the biggest needs was for better information about care services in languages other than English.

'Some of the things we are suggesting will cost absolutely nothing, only thought and sensitivity,' he said.

© The Guardian
August, 1996

British Pensioners' Charter

As amended by the 1993 Biennial Conference of British Pensioners and Trade Union Action Association

1. A universal basic state retirement pension of not less than 1/3 of average earnings for each pensioner, 60 to be the universal retiring age for women and men for them to be eligible for the full state pension.

2. Full health care provision including hospital and community care shall be free and available at time of need and where needed.

3. Payments of an additional £5 a week heating allowance to all pensioner households from October 1st to March 31st each year.

4. Christmas bonus of £50 to be paid to all pensioners, free of Income Tax.

5. The death grant to be restored and renamed, more appropriately, the Funeral Grant and to be in the sum of £600.00

6. All payments to pensioners to be uprated at 6-monthly intervals on the basis of the increase in earnings or the cost of living, whichever is the greater.

7. All pensioner households to be relieved of paying standing charges and for TV licences.

8. Free travel facilities to be available for all pensioners on bus, coach, underground and rail services, whether publicly or privately owned, nationwide. Equal facilities to be available for disabled pensioners.

9. All pensioners to be able to live in accommodation which is appropriate to personal needs and circumstances including sheltered housing, with life-line facilities.

10. The full range of social and community services to be available to pensioners as and when needed. Pensioners to be entitled to Invalid Care Allowance.

11. SERPS to be restored to its original form and occupational pension schemes to be completely independent of employers and to be under the control of trustees composed of at least 50% elected worker representatives and with alternating chairmanships.

● This Charter is issued by the British Pensioners' & T.U. Action Association, 315 Bexley Road, Erith, Kent, from whom further copies may be obtained. © British Pensioners' & T.U. Action Association

Scientists find clues to prolonged life

By Tom Wilkie, Science Editor

A gene that controls ageing has been found by US researchers, raising the possibility that gene therapy or drugs might prolong active human life to 150 years.

By isolating and identifying the gene, researchers hope they may be able to devise treatments that could slow the process of ageing.

A team led by Dr Gerard Schellenberg at the Veterans' Health Care System, in Seattle, reports the gene's discovery in today's issue of the US journal *Science*.

They discovered the gene by looking at people with Werner's syndrome – a form of premature ageing – which results from inheriting an abnormal variant of the gene. There are an estimated 1,000 people with Werner's syndrome in Britain, according to Professor Sydney Shall, an expert on the disease at Sussex University. The average age of death is 45, but some last until their 50s.

Professor Shall suggested Werner's syndrome may have been the primordial human standard, while 'normal' people evolved the extra gene to acquire our present longevity.

The gene appears to slow ageing. 'What if we put in another one?' he asked. 'One hundred and fifty years is not an unreasonable human life-span and we are talking about healthy, vigorous life.'

Scientists have already transplanted genes to correct inherited diseases, such as cystic fibrosis. Transplanting a gene to affect ageing would be an extension of this process.

People with Werner's develop normally until they are about 10, when they stop growing. By their 30s they have severe arteriosclerosis – narrowing of the arteries associated with old age and can develop

diabetes, cancer, osteoporosis and rheumatoid arthritis. 'They look twice as old as they really are,' Professor Shall said.

Body cells taken from patients with Werner's syndrome have 'dramatic and odd' limitations when cultured in the laboratory. They stop growing about five or six times faster than normal cells.

'The positive function of the gene is to keep cells growing for a much longer time,' Professor Shall said.

The identification of the gene will also allow parents to have a prenatal diagnosis where there is a risk to a foetus.

© *The Independent*
April, 1996

Needs of the elderly 'will control EU'

By Toby Helm, EU Correspondent in Brussels

The number of people aged over 60 in the European Union will rise by almost 50 per cent to 113.5 million by 2025, creating communities 'dominated by the needs of older people', according to a European Commission study.

The most comprehensive report yet on future demographic trends in the EU gives a warning of 'an explosion in the number of people approaching retirement'.

It says that the financial burden of supporting rapidly rising elderly populations will be even more severe because the number of young people and those of working age will drop markedly over the same period. By 2025 the number of people under 20 will fall by 11 per cent, and the number of adults aged between 20 and 59 will drop by 6.4 per cent.

The Commission suggests investigating the potential spending savings from raising pension ages in response to the huge increase in costs.

© *The Daily Telegraph plc*
London, 1996

INDEX

ADDITIONAL RESOURCES

You might like to contact the following organisations for further information. Due to the increasing cost of postage, many organisations cannot respond to enquiries unless they receive a stamped, addressed envelope.

Age Concern England
Astral House
London, SW16 4ER
Tel: 0181 679 8000
Age Concern provides a comprehensive information service, produces an extensive list of publications, and runs a wide range of training courses.

Age Concern Cymru
4th Floor
1 Cathedral Road
Cardiff, CF1 9SD
Tel: 01222 371566
Fax: 01222 399562

Age Concern Northern Ireland
3 Lower Crescent
Belfast, BT7 1NR
Tel: 01232 245729
Fax: 01232 235497

Age Concern Scotland
54a Fountainbridge
Edinburgh, EH3 9PT
Tel: 0131 228 5656
Fax: 0131 228 5416
Publishes a wide range of factsheets, leaflets and books.

Association of Retired Persons
Greencoat House
Francis Street
London, SW1P 1DZ
Tel: 0171 895 8880
Fax: 0171 233 7132
A national association representing. They produce a bi-monthly magazine and newspaper and 24-hour legal and domestic helplines with a wide range of social activities. Publishes *ARP 050*, a magazine for the retired.

British Pensioners & Trade Union Action Association (BPTUAA)
51 Hampton Drive
Newport
Shropshire, TF10 7RE

Centre for Policy on Ageing
25-31 Ironmongers Row

London, EC1V 3QP
Tel: 0171 253 1787
Fax: 0171 490 4206
An independent organisation which aims to raise issues of public importance on matters to do with ageing and old age. They produce publications.

Counsel and Care
Twyman House
16 Bonny Street
London, NW1 9PG
Tel: 0171 485 1566
Gives free and confidential advice to older people, carers and professionals such as social workers. Produces publications including a range of factsheets relating to care for older people.

Department for Education and Employment (DFEE)
Caxton House
Tothill Street
London, SW1H 9NT
Tel: 0171 273 5325
Produces *Age Works*

Employers Forum on Age
Astral House
London, SW16 4ER
Tel: 0181 679 8000
A network of leading employers deriving benefit from a mixed age workforce. Recently published *Age and Employment: Why Employers should think again about Older Workers*. Price £14:95.

Help the Aged
St James' Walk
London, EC1R 0BE
Tel: 0171 253 0253
Aims to improve the quality of life for elderly people in the UK. Ask for their publication list.

The Industrial Society
Robert Hyde House
48 Bryanston Square
London, W1H 7LN
Tel: 0171 262 2401

Produces range of booklets and information packs on work related topics including: working mothers, racial and sexual harassment and age related issues.

Joseph Rowntree Foundation
The Homestead
40 Water End
York, YO3 6LP
Tel: 01904 629241
The Foundation is an independent, non-political body which funds programmes of research and innovative development in the fields of housing, social care and social policy.

Pensioners' Voice
14 Peter Street
Blackburn
Lancashire, BB2 2HD
Tel: 01254 52606
Well known pressure group for people who are over 50. It has over 400 branches in the UK.

Research into Ageing
15-17 St Cross Street
London, EC1N 8UN
Tel: 0171 404 6878
Fax: 0171 404 6816
A registered charity which publishes a wide range of material aimed at those working with older people and for academics and students studying social work and social gerontology. Suitable for further and higher education studies.

Trade Union Congress – Equal Rights Department
Congress House
23-28 Great Russell Street
London, WC1B 3LS
Tel: 0171 636 4030
Fax: 0171 636 0632
The TUC is a federation of British trade unions. They publish several factsheets on pensions: price 35p each. Ask for their publication list.

ACKNOWLEDGEMENTS

The publisher is grateful for permission to reproduce the following material.

While every care has been taken to trace and acknowledge copyright, the publisher tenders its apology for any accidental infringement or where copyright has proved untraceable. The publisher would be pleased to come to a suitable arrangement in any such case with the rightful owner.

Chapter One: Age Discrimination

Advice and help for older people, © Counsel and Care, *Campaign for older workers*, © Campaign for Older Workers, *Age discrimination*, © Industrial Society, *There are worse injustices than 'ageism'*, © The Independent, May 1996, *Is this the right time to be tackling the age issue?*, © Employers Forum on Age (EFA), *Ageism*, © Help the Aged, *Keep young and employable*, © The Independent, February 1996, *Age works*, © The Department for Education and Employment, *Ageism ban ushers in new jobs era for older workers*, © The Daily Mail, July 1996.

Chapter Two: The Economics of Ageing

The poverty debate, © Help the Aged, *Income*, © Help the Aged, *Poverty awaits those who fail to save up for their retirement*, © The Guardian, September 1996, *Europe faces a grey future*, © The Guardian, March 1996, *Why didn't you save more, Grandpa?*, © The Independent, January 1996, *Older people in the United Kingdom*, © Age Concern, *Your pensions options*, © Trades Union Congress, *Your pension*, © ARP 050.

Chapter Three: Retirement

The retired population, © Help the Aged, *Thinking about early retirement?*, © Trades Union Congress, *Nobody called*, © The Guardian, July 1995, *Britain 'facing crisis' over care of the elderly*, © The Telegraph plc, London 1996, *Myth of the 'geriatric timebomb' is exploded*, © The Telegraph plc, London 1996, *Value of home 'should fund care in old age'*, © The Independent, January 1996, *Paying for residential care*, © British Pensioners' and Trade Union Association, Summer 1996, *Paying for nursing homes*, © The Guardian, May 1996, *Meeting the cost of continuing care*, © Joseph Rowntree Foundation, April 1996, *Créche takes grannies back to childhood*, © The Independent, May 1996, *Slow: Fun-loving OAPs ahead*, © The Daily Mail, August 1996, *Greying population stays in the pink*, © New Scientist, March 1996, *Laughter really is the best medicine*, © The Daily Mail, August 1996, *Family care 'lacking for elderly blacks and Asians'*, © The Guardian, August 1996, *British Pensioners' Charter*, © British Pensioners' and Trade Union Association, *Scientists find clues to prolonged life*, © The Independent, April 1996, *Needs of the elderly 'will control EU'*, © The Telegraph plc, London 1996.

Photographs and Illustrations

Pages 1, 6: Katherine Fleming / Folio Collective, pages 11, 12, 23, 34: Ken Pyne, pages 15, 27, 37: Andrew Smith / Folio Collective.

Craig Donnellan
Cambridge
January, 1997